CW01272252

This version of Decision Making in Uncertain Times was first published in 2023

© 2023 by Tony Fish

Peak Paradox grants the following to anyone who wants to use the content in this book. Creative Commons license: Attribution-NonCommercial-ShareAlike.

This means you are free to read it, play with it, mix it, flip it, adapt it, build on it or mash it together; we just ask that you reference it back to this book, acknowledging Peak Paradox and the author. Please go and have some fun with the thinking in this book, it was a joy to create and write. We are looking forward to learning from all those who carry it forward.

CC BY-NC-SA

This license lets you remix, adapt, and build upon this work, non-commercially, as long as you credit Peak Paradox and onwards license your new creations under identical terms.

The License in Overview • Legal Terms of the License

Hardback 978-1-7384227-3-9
Paperback 978-1-7384227-0-8
Kindle 978-1-7384227-1-5
EPUB 978-1-7384227-2-2

Making fire

You are the expert in your own experience, and my working assumption is that I cannot and would not know if there is anything I can bring to you that is profound or revolutionary about decision making in uncertain times. I don't know your individual background, insights from the life of hard knocks, or earned wisdom. Therefore, I would never presume that in a one-hour seminar, a one-day coaching session, or an immersion chapter of this book, I could teach you anything about how you should change something to make better decisions. However, if I get the articulation of my flow right, when you read this book, you will glean something that nobody can tell you how to find or touch. Concepts will emerge as you combine your unique perspective with my flow, and you will create new thinking and insights.

In presenting these ten concepts about decision making in uncertain times, the intention is not that I want you to think like me, or that by reading this work you will have the solution to decision-making in uncertain times. I want you always to think like you do but have reflected, learnt or honed something about your own framing. This will happen as the book creates sparks, but not agreement. Alignment feels good but leads to group thinking, so I desire that we co-create fire. Like two flints hitting each other to make a spark, your experience and my flow should collide. I will achieve my objective, and value will be created as you realise that you are the fuel.

My ask is that when those sparks create goosebumps, you share them with others so that we can all learn from your insights, as this is the oxygen. Together, we will have created a trinity of purifying fire to improve decision-making in uncertain times. Ignition, fuel and oxygen. Fire will provide much of what we need for our journey; however, it takes time to build a fire, and we should therefore take enough time to find the dry tinder, the right kindling and quality fuel.

This chapter provides a map to navigate the journey and explains why there is a need to find connections and understand the gaps within, and appreciate the beauty of, complex relationships - starting with purpose and strategy. It starts to reveal my flow; you should not agree with it all or how will we create sparks to ignite fire?

The relationship between purpose and strategy

Purpose emerges from the combination of a profession (skills crafted by nature and nurture), passion (unsuppressed natural alignment, seen as easy and enjoyable) and concepts of altruism (that which makes the world better.) Profession and passion are measurable, bounded and can be qualified; altruism is unbounded, unmeasurable, cultural, contextual, and subjective. Our understanding of what makes the world better is the dynamic aspect of purpose which means every individual and generation gets to reimagine purpose based on better knowledge, skills and previous experiences.

For an individual, their purpose has to lose its purity as it is eroded by the compromises needed to function in society. Individuals have to embrace collective or group purposes and business purposes to be able to work. Therefore, we should recognise that our individual, group or business purposes can either become aligned, co-created and in harmony (happy place) or misaligned, destructive and in conflict (stress from compromises).

The concept of a strategy is how we get from the here and now to where an individual or group perceives the future, based on an agreeable purpose. However, this depends on the analysis of available data and is constrained by the accessible resources. We have to face that for many reasons, the jump is often too far from today's reality to an imagined future, so we infill with the concepts of aims, goals and an overarching mission. These concepts enable better articulation to find agreeable and achievable objectives. They act as stepping stones to open up influential short-term and long-term strategic thinking concepts.

When we reflect on the many drawings, diagrams and images representing the relationships between purpose, vision, mission and strategy, they tend to feel rigid, linear and static. Interlaced circles, spirals, triangles, and flowing blocks do not capture the vivid imagination of the dynamic, pulsating, messy, intertwingled and evolving relationship that connects purpose and strategy. Our one-dimensional representations of these connections and relationships suck out the energy and excitement, and we are forced to focus on watered-down articulations out of immediate demand for action to meet short-term objectives. Decision making in a multidimensional world differs from the choices we face in the supermarket.

Our understanding of the relationship between purpose (**why**) and strategy (**how**) has always been important and will remain so. We know our appreciation of the relationship expands as we collect more knowledge and experience, but in times of change (political, economic, social, technical, or legal), when new ideas are emerging, or when there is increased volatility and uncertainty, we must reflect to confirm or reassess whether our **why** and **how** are still relevant.

There is a natural movement from **why** and **how** to focus on who, which demands that we explore **what** is changing. We should hold close an appreciation that our understanding of these relationships grows as we do.

> This book is about decision making in uncertain times. The decisions in focus in this book are both the why and how decisions and the complex, interwoven relationships between them. Additionally, we must accept the consequences of the decisions others have made on the choices we now face.

Strategy is not a game of chess

Strategy and strategic thinking are often elevated to be considered as the most important thing in business; therefore, the word "strategy" invokes a vast range of thinking and an equal number of responses.

Some prefer that strategy is the reserve of leaders, the elite and the greatest commanders, but in my view, this is a propagated lie derived from fear, power and control. If you have delegated purpose, you have forfeited your right to determine strategy. Strategy is complex and hard when you don't have a clear and agreed purpose; many prefer the superiority this pretence affords to getting deep and dirty into resolving the reasons for existence (the purpose).

Alternatively, strategy can be tossed around like a common soft toy as if easy, simple and requiring no deep insights, enabling the misconception that a simple BCG or McKinsey quadrant matrix or one-page strategy exercise is all you need. Ultimately, strategy has more similarity to beauty, trust and truth, where the eye of the beholder determines the outcome, than to the immovable laws of physics, mountains, or a mother's love. Because purpose influences strategy, and how we deliver strategy determines the next generation's ideals of purpose, we cannot escape the dependencies.

That said, strategy is about determining the acceptable plan most likely to achieve agreed on long-term goals within the context of a market, constraints and uncertainty. You can read this as a right to make decisions. Strategy can undoubtedly be simplified when there are no constraints, limits or conflicting requirements, and the historical records are a near-perfect predictor of the future.

Such a situation occurs when we are naive or persuaded that there is high stability and certainty in the long run. Strategy can never be simplistic and uncomplicated; in the same way, purpose cannot only be passion. Passion, you will remember from the opening, is one of the three foundations.

This book is about decision making in uncertain times. The decisions in focus in this book are both the why and how decisions, and the book unpacks when and why we overly simplify some decisions and overly complicate others.

Finite but dynamic

Everything is finite, but some things are here for longer than others. The Earth is finite, but the period between forming and collapsing is so vast it appears infinite to human life. Decisions are finite, but some remain relevant and applicable for longer than others.

Human physical life is finite, started by birth and truncated by death. The life span for an individual is hopefully 80 years, and only for a limited period in this span can we lift our thinking above short-term needs to consider a purpose for a better world, something beyond and outside of our own finite limitations. Legacies of being a better ancestor, a business, or a collective memory of an individual, can all survive beyond a lived-life. As the actual memory of an individual fades, their worthy or noble purpose and enterprise with meaning, if up-to-date and current, will remain.

Mayflies have the shortest lifespan on Earth, lasting 24 hours; human life appears infinite to them. Yes, pre-mayfly nymphs can exist for two years, but the only purpose of the mayfly stage of the insect lifecycle is reproduction, which is very time limited. In that tiny period of being a mayfly, the insect has to fulfil a single purpose and create something less finite - the next generation - from something finite. All living biological things need to optimise for a single purpose at some point in their life patterns, fundamentally for long-term survival, with adaptation being part of a short-term strategy to support long-term thriving (**note**: not control or domination).

At the opening of this book, I said, "Purpose (individual) emerges from the combination of your profession (what you are good at, crafted by nature and nurture), passion (what you find easy and enjoy) and what makes the world better." Reproduction is where nature provides an overwhelming and obvious singular purpose which may only align for a short period; hence our purpose has to be more dynamic. Single purposes such as survival make us finite, much like data does, as we will begin to unpack.

As one species adapts to a new environment aligned with its survival purpose, it changes the environment for the others, who now have to adapt. Species need to adapt because something else created the change in their environment. Purpose is dynamic, and it creates dynamics. We see this in a long-term dynamic predator-prey model or in the ebbs and flows of competitive outcomes in a free market. Emperor penguins appear to have one aim during the harsh winter, a hard-coded purpose: "get to the centre." This single purpose in a large colony of penguins creates a continually changing raft that can move miles as each penguin tries to get to the centre, because the purpose is to keep warm (connected) and survive by sharing the realities of a harsh outer boundary.

Companies are finite, first founded and then wound up. There is nothing to stop a company from living forever as they are not bound by human frailties, just by economics; but, the average lifespan of companies continually falls[1]. A killer of companies and species is finite behaviour; this is seen as being unable to adapt or be dynamic (possessing static skills) and not acting as anti-finite.

Adam Smith warned us in 1776 of the consequences of a company's power, when, in its construction, it has an unlimited life (if it is dynamic and can adapt), unlimited licence (no boundary), unlimited size and unlimited power; this frames why a company's purpose and culture are so critical, as they create boundaries. Further, as companies don't have owners on their own, a company has no ability to determine that the written purpose is a good one. Humans craft the purpose, forge the culture and are responsible for the subsequent ethical or unethical decisions. This framing of an unlimited existence is the same reality of many AI and ethics discussions, which is why so much time is afforded to data, and its impact on decision making, in this book. To the point companies don't have owners, yes, they have shareholders, but shareholders are not owners. A company owns itself - but don't trust me, search for it. Start your search with "who owns a company?" This is important because when we think we know the answer, we ignore the choices made.

---

[1] https://www.statista.com/statistics/1259275/average-company-lifespan/

I present frameworks that are driven by a concept of **#Anti-Finite** as something that we need to build on, and that these are closer in concept to that of anti-fragile[2] from Nassim Nicholas Taleb than Infinite Games[3] from Simon Sinek - although I love both these books. How we craft decisions based on anti-finite ideals, a dynamic purpose to overcome being finite, is foundational to being a better ancestor and thinking about the impact of decisions on future generations.

As a leader, you will know that your company's purpose results from previous leadership. The refinement or determination of a new purpose is the remit of the existing leadership. The company's leadership and people influence its culture and help determine its strategy; these, in turn, impact and help determine the dynamic nature of its purpose. Back to how we imagine the colourful abstraction of intertwingled relationships between purpose and strategy.

It should be evident that a leadership team that is static (repeat last year + x%) or one-dimensional (single objective, such as shareholder primacy) will make the finite, finite. Whereas leaders who are embracing holistic concepts of ecosystem equality, climate responsibilities, integrated and systems thinking, and being better ancestors, are demonstrating the dynamics required to make the finite endure. Leadership in this regard may be in conflict with shareholders and other stakeholders. Some areas of leadership focus, such as becoming digital, are merely an adaptation; often one-dimensional, and to be absolutely clear, not a purpose or a strategy.

If an aspect of the company director's role is to ensure the company's long-term success, then we have to be anti-finite and exist where resilience, robustness and agility meet. This place is messy, and the question we have to dwell on is, "How do we make better decisions?"

> **This book is about decision making in uncertain times. The decisions in focus in this book are both the why and how decisions and how we can develop and build anti-finite thinking that will provide an advantage in framing decision making, enabling us to thrive in times of increased uncertainty.**

---

[2] Anti-fragile reveals how some systems thrive from shocks, volatility and uncertainty instead of breaking from them, and how you can adapt more anti-fragile traits yourself to thrive in an uncertain and chaotic world.

[3] The Infinite Game explores leadership choices and provides guidelines to implement an "infinite game" plan. Finite mindsets focus on winning, whereas infinite mindsets develop a more significant cause than ourselves or our business.

Does purpose need a Northstar?

Whilst a purpose makes sense at scale from the perspective of an individual, the same purpose as "reason or rationale" for a company or community is full of paradoxes, as each individual will bring their interpretation and translation. We appear unable to agree on one unified "Human Purpose," and as insufficient resources are available to optimise for everything that everyone wants, we must determine where best to allocate resources.

Economists realise that there are numerous "purposes" that we can allocate our resources (time, money) to realise what we think or believe is important. In a company context, our choices and decisions are full of paradoxes and dilemmas for ourselves and for those who feel the consequences of our decisions. We are left with the reality that even with a purpose, we often get decisions wrong; sometimes, because of the wrong data or compromise, perhaps incentives changed behaviour, or because the purpose should have been updated. As we allocate limited resources, we will be held responsible and accountable by our fiduciary duty, which is to act in the best interests of all stakeholders (s.172 of the UK Companies Act); for this, we may look for a Northstar.

A Northstar allows us to optimise in seemingly the same direction and be together on the same journey, but without being prescriptive. A Northstar enables a purpose to be dynamic and breathe. In agreeing on a Northstar, we become more aligned, heading towards a single optimised ideal, which is at the expense of other equally valued ideals.

"Smart management" and "smart leaders" apparently make yearly resolutions and set quarterly milestones, charting progress against ambitious plans and goals. Meanwhile, "wise leaders" build from a foundation with a purpose that creates a compelling vision, therefore creating action — not just for that year, but for the rest of their finite lives. Purpose helps find and lock onto a Northstar; this Northstar provides light when the finite life of the instigator has finished or the path ahead is hazy, humility when arrogance announces false victory, and inspiration when the outlook seems bleak.

To fulfil purpose, we must find a team that aligns with the compromises we have to make. Individuals find some compromises easier than others, for reasons that are often difficult to explain. When we aim for a Northstar, the journey is easier and more agreeable if those on the journey align with the compromises, and we form a unified team. This does not mean group-think or that we have to agree; dissent is still the most valued opinion. However, as teams grow, we inevitably shift, and must also focus on bringing in new skills and experience, using past performance as a primary measure for recruitment. This process dilutes the clarity of purpose and Northstar alignment and loses sight of the compromises we agreed on. Suddenly, we find that those on our journey have different purposes, incentives, compromises and strategic imperatives. These differences create tensions, conflicts and stresses that break the model, our team, and ourselves.

With dilution comes that feeling of being forced into a decision or compromise that does not align with your purpose/strategy. That sense of unease will not go away as the data or something you instinctively know tells you that you have moved away from the desired path in the pretence of a better outcome.

Whilst we cannot touch, see or feel what it is that frustrates us and holds us back, in such times we know that we would like something that helps us gain clarity and understanding. As a leader, you must search out the paradoxes in the data to gain clarity in your decision making. Being unable to find them means you remain in someone else's framing and model, losing your grip on the reality that you are optimising for. The "Peak Paradox" framework presented in the final chapter provides a tool to unpick the compromises being forced by a certain decision.

> This book is about decision making in uncertain times, and regardless of how much data analysis, information, and insight is available, there is usually more than one possible outcome or direction, even with a clear purpose. The following chapters frame and identify systems and processes, and how these can work to undermine good decisions and judgments that management and leadership teams make. The frameworks presented in this book are designed to shine a light on why some decisions do not create purpose-aligned outcomes, by clarifying the compromises each of us brings to a team decision. What is truly unique is that "Peak Paradox" helps unpack why this is happening without creating tension or conflict.

As to having a vision and mission!

You may have noticed that I have thus far avoided the words "vision" and "mission".

Having "vision" is the ability to think about or plan the future with imagination or wisdom. An individual with a clear vision can appear evolutionary, revolutionary, or out of touch with reality. Vision, like purpose, functions conceptually at an individual level, but falls apart at the scale required in business due to the inherent tensions, conflicts and compromises created by those in a leadership capacity.

Popularised in the 1990s by management consultants and theorists, a "vision statement" is an insufferable description which purports a direction that aligns with an underlying philosophy. Vision statements should set out the company's ambitious idea, based on imagination and wisdom, and communicate how this would make a difference. Vision statements worthy of note - in my view, right now, there are none. Search for "leading examples of vision statements" and dwell on them. Find your own company's vision statement and reflect on it. Does your vision statement articulate the future with imagination or wisdom, or describe how you will make the world a better place? Importantly, does it align with your principles?

Mission statements, the counterpart to vision statements, became ubiquitous during the 1980s, when Peter Drucker and others popularised them as a way for companies to articulate a summary of the company purpose. However, Milton Friedman's corrupted ideals regarding the sole purpose of an organisation, that were popularised as "shareholder primacy", meant that many mission statements have become defined as action-based statements confirming the blend between the two big purpose ideas for companies. These are serving a customer, and shareholder, primacy; thus setting out an organisation's allegiance to shareholder returns and how they can "exploit" customers as the goal to deliver it.

We appear to have confused and morphed concepts of purpose and Northstar into vision and mission statements, and, in doing so, we have given up the structure and framework for making better decisions.

Additionally, there are no means for reflection to ask if we are doing the right thing. We live in an economic and financial framing where efficiency and effectiveness trump efficacy, in decision making.

Now, you could interpret my positioning (morphed concepts of purpose and Northstar to vision and mission statements) as favouring governance and strategy via principle and rule-based frameworks over "doing something". However, there is a difference between "decide what the act is" and "action to confirm what to decide". The former, "decide what the act is", takes the decision on a course of action and then commits to it. Whereas the latter, "action to confirm what to decide", fosters small moves intended to reduce risk and improve possibilities until choices become limited to one that is now overwhelmingly attractive, enabling commitment. There is much debate among commentaries as to which of the two approaches is more effective in uncertain and unpredictable environments. Both have merits and faults, supporters and dissenters. You will sense in the different chapters that I bias towards one approach and, in another chapter, the alternative. It is not undecidedness but rather the need to use every tool. The reason for this is that risk is not probability, and neither is uncertainty.

> This book is about decision making in uncertain times and will require you to rethink leadership and management tools which were right at the time, easy to teach, and provided shortcuts, but which may not have longevity. Our bias towards what we know and hold to be true may not help us make the right decision.

Dynamic governance

Governance is not new, and when the thinking first emerged that we needed oversight about decisions others take, the world was full of different demands and power structures. Governance for many is finite, but to remain relevant, it must be anti-finite; governance should be dynamic and adaptable. We know that new governance thinking will be built on the best aspects of everything we have thought of and created so far. Whilst we will take the foundations of the original thinking and add in learning and wisdom of where we have got to, we have to acknowledge that this will not be enough to establish governance that will be fit for the next 1000 years, because the systems we have to govern with must also be transformed.

We must build on (not lose) the original governance ideas regarding agreeing on a Northstar and finding purpose. We must keep at the core a requirement that the director's role is to question if the Northstar is still the place to be heading towards. We must develop the thinking that we should continually steer a course to the Northstar (and that can mean going south for a while), and that the directors are responsible for short and long-term adjustments on the journey.

These two foundational stones, Northstar and Journey, remain valid and dependable. We can take the best of c. 20th century thinking as pillars, which includes checks and balances to ensure that we are making the right adjustments on our journey and that our vessel (aka the ship that represented our company in the original analogy) is in the right order. Indeed, have we got the right vessel to be able to continue the journey?

However, just applying the thinking of foundations and pillars ignores the fact that we are now in a hyper-dependent, emergent, complex and adaptive ecosystem, and we have to become better ancestors by moving to become environmentally sustainable.

We cannot afford to leave behind a burnt Earth for our grandchildren just because we want to get to our Northstar at any cost. This does not mean new governance ideals of being a better ancestor will last forever; it just states that our next requirement of governance is that it must remain dynamic and avoid the confines of compliance.

Figure 1: Governance for the next 1000 years

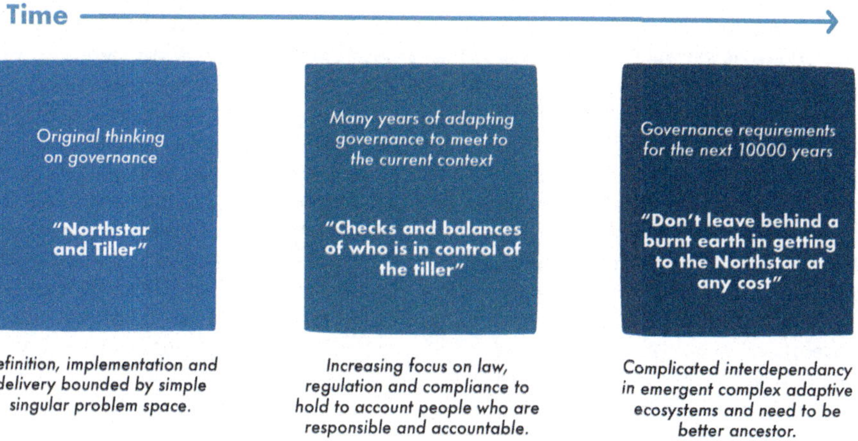

Time ⟶

Original thinking on governance	Many years of adapting governance to meet to the current context	Governance requirements for the next 10000 years
"Northstar and Tiller"	"Checks and balances of who is in control of the tiller"	"Don't leave behind a burnt earth in getting to the Northstar at any cost"
Definition, implementation and delivery bounded by simple singular problem space.	Increasing focus on law, regulation and compliance to hold to account people who are responsible and accountable.	Complicated interdependancy in emergent complex adaptive ecosystems and need to be better ancestor.

We left a long time ago a market where our value, purpose or mission had no other dependencies or dependents. Value chains were popularised in the 1980/90s, but by 2020 we became fully immersed in ecosystems. Within our ecosystem, the shared Northstar can be closer or further away than others with whom we have co-dependencies. Indeed, we can have very different Northstars from our geographically diverse dependent suppliers and customers, who may not need to be aligned with our direction or journey. However, we depend on them for data, products/services, and income.

The complexity of the high dependency present in our market has built efficiency and brittleness simultaneously. Brittleness means less ability to adapt/change, and that we can be steered off course – not by our actions, but through the automated governance closed-loop system (compliance) that we have built for efficiency and effectiveness over efficacy. The emergence of complexity within the systems is beyond one person's understanding, shattering the concept of a leader being a single entity. Therefore, we need to find new ways of bringing data to the directors and leadership teams to help make better judgement/decisions and deliver governance.

We must recognise that the economic prosperity that we enjoy, and that our companies have been built on, depends on "free" (uncosted) resources which provide the ability not to worry, do not require us to cost them or to be concerned with the short or long-term effects. As we recognise the impact of humans on our Earth, we also can see that the next generation cannot journey on the same path as previous generations, including ours. We, together with our grandparents and parents, have burnt that path. We have used the resources without due care for generations to come, and left behind so much waste that the same journey would be toxic. Therefore, we must add far more than ESG data to governance and become more proactive about being good ancestors. To be good ancestors, directors must be held accountable and responsible for their actions.

To do this, we must have better oversight and governance, which is not more of the same, but something new. What would change if your decisions followed you and did not remain behind the "confidential" door of the company you left? Transparency on the provenance and lineage of data, and availability of data about decisions made, is going to be critical. What we report on, how we report, how we make decisions, and what the outcomes of our decisions are, are dependent on data – and this information is also data. This data helps us improve our judgement, so we must find ways to test and secure the data's lineage and provenance. We must be able to share data and decisions so that we can improve, not at our own rate but at an exponential rate, the potential for all humans to contribute to better outcomes for our children.

> This book is about decision making in uncertain times, and we should acknowledge that decisions come from choices. If we are not capable of finding choices that align with our Northstar and purpose, decision making becomes futile and leads to a finite ending. In everything we do, we need to ensure that good governance, with the necessary oversight and compliance controls, and that questions those who are responsible, is in place.

The board agenda

The board is the place where we wrestle and struggle with decisions in uncertain times. The board should be the most human space in a company. The board must have a vantage point to ensure the widest possible perspective.

The board should be guided by data, rules, our values, and our principles; and be considerate and question others' values, principles and behaviours, to sanity check our perspective. The board needs clarity of tasks, processes, strategy, and purpose, with a Northstar as a guide.

Figure 2: A board must take a vantage point, so that it can ensure the widest possible perspective

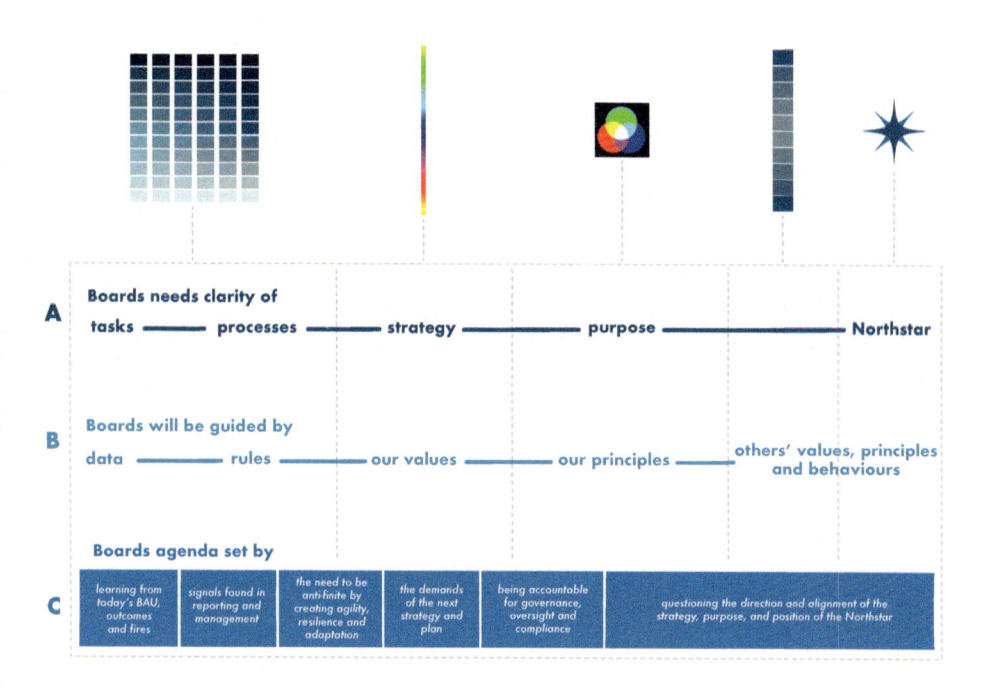

A — Boards needs clarity of
tasks — processes — strategy — purpose — Northstar

B — Boards will be guided by
data — rules — our values — our principles — others' values, principles and behaviours

C — Boards agenda set by
- learning from today's BAU, outcomes and fires
- signals found in reporting and management
- the need to be anti-finite by creating agility, resilience and adaptation
- the demands of the next strategy and plan
- being accountable for governance, oversight and compliance
- questioning the direction and alignment of the strategy, purpose, and position of the Northstar

The demand for clarity and guidance should create a wide-ranging board agenda where the team learns from today's BAU (Business As Usual), outcomes, and fires being fought on the front line. This board should be capable of picking up small signals in the noise of day-to-day reporting and management demands. Critically, the board needs to set a culture that has agility, resilience, and can be adaptive, so that it can be anti-finite. The agenda should include the next strategic plan, and provide a safe space for criticism, dynamic governance and compliance. Finally, the board should question its purpose, see if the Northstar is still the right one, and determine if there is an alignment between strategy, purpose, and the Northstar. The important point here is that board agendas that remain set by function will repeat the same, and are therefore doomed to failure. In many of the chapters, I will force you to consider data and the flows of information. You will come to question how we should confirm attestation.

There are increasingly more factors to consider in decision making and board work, most of which are material, but many that are not directly observable or visible through a finance lens. The presence of these factors is felt through their effects, and we will only improve the effects if we can ask better questions. To paraphrase Richard Feynman, *give me questions I cannot answer, and not answers I cannot question.*

> **This book is about decision making in uncertain times. The decisions in focus in this book are both the why and how decisions, and the content is set out to challenge and make you think, so that you may become more aware of the importance of a board and a directorship role.**
>
> ***The purpose of this book is also to help you form better questions!***

It is now time to get deep and dirty into the cauldron to create some sparks, make the fire, and boil up some new magic.

How to read this book

Increasingly, leadership teams must contend with volatility, which creates more uncertainty. Instability in markets creates data that is noisy, messy and complex. Thus, business decisions become more challenging to analyse and forecast.

While our critical decision intent is often well-founded, rapidly changing externalities, bias, and out-of-date internal processes mean that our decisions create unintended consequences; challenging our business models and changing our risk profile, often without us knowing.

Given that ambiguous and uncomfortable data is easy to ignore, how do we improve our decision-making capacity? If "How do I make better decisions in uncertain times" is the question, the clarification is "so that I can be more aware of the future consequences of my decisions".

The content presented in this book is principally aimed at senior leadership, executives, board members, NEDs and directors, as it demands a level of exposure and experience. However, it is of equal value for those who aspire to take on one of these roles.

Unfortunately, the linear form of a book is not ideal for unpacking the complexity of decision making, so here is the reality - this is not a book. Presented are 6 major concepts that constitute a continuous circular flow. Each concept has deep dependencies and relationships with the others. This is a linear narrative, explaining circular concepts of complexity and intertwingularity, and this book will help you to improve your decision making by giving you new capabilities and expertise.

What you can expect from this book

This book aims to provide you with:

- An improvement in your understanding of evidence, proof and truthfulness of data presented; determination of how you are being framed.

- A new ability to question "data" experts; and determine the consequences on outcomes using different analyses with the same data.

The diagram below shows the linkage between the chapters; the hash numbers (#1 to 10) are the chapters' order and focus. Over half the chapters focus on unpacking the processes and decision-making methods with data (action), and the remaining half on making better decisions (reflection).

Figure 3: How to read this book

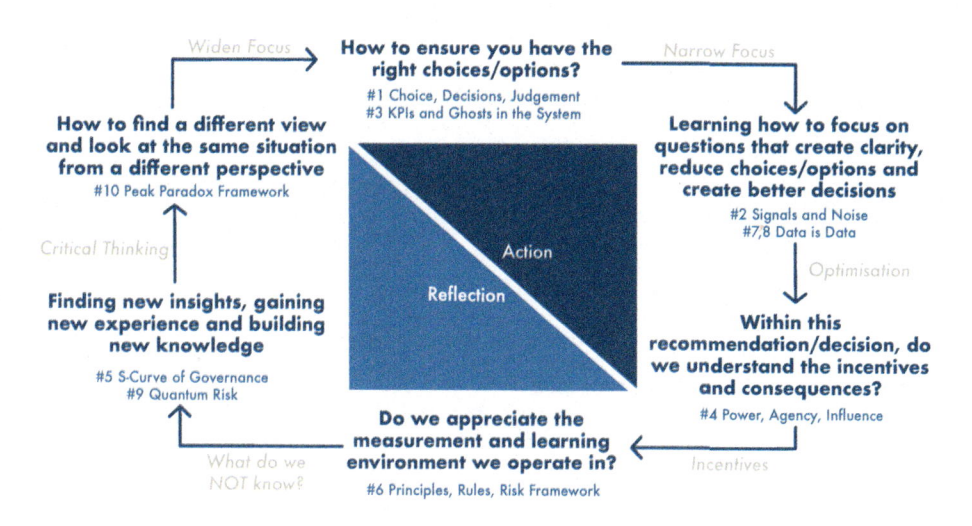

Widen Focus

How to ensure you have the right choices/options?
#1 Choice, Decisions, Judgement
#3 KPIs and Ghosts in the System

Narrow Focus

How to find a different view and look at the same situation from a different perspective
#10 Peak Paradox Framework

Learning how to focus on questions that create clarity, reduce choices/options and create better decisions
#2 Signals and Noise
#7,8 Data is Data

Critical Thinking

Action

Reflection

Optimisation

Finding new insights, gaining new experience and building new knowledge
#5 S-Curve of Governance
#9 Quantum Risk

Within this recommendation/decision, do we understand the incentives and consequences?
#4 Power, Agency, Influence

What do we NOT know?

Do we appreciate the measurement and learning environment we operate in?
#6 Principles, Rules, Risk Framework

Incentives

Contents

i	*Making fire*	*(Page 3)*
ii	*How to read this book*	*(Page 18)*
iii	*What you can expect from this book*	*(Pages 19)*

Chapter 1 — Choice, decision making and judgement
Page 24 — *Is your relationship constructive or destructive?*

Chapter 2 — The Shadowy Hierarchy
Page 38 — *What prevents us from making better decisions?*

Chapter 3 — Are KPIs the nemesis of innovation?
Page 56 — *Applying data effectively in order to grow*

Chapter 4 — Power, agency and influence
Page 68 — *A new framework about complex relationships*

Chapter 5 — Revising the S-curve in an age of emergence
Page 78 — *Exploring how the S-curve can help us with leadership*

Chapter 6 — Humans want principles, society demands rules and businesses want to manage risk
Page 92 — *Can we reconcile the differences?*

Chapter 7 — Data; evidence and proof
Page 108 — *1) Data is Data*
Page 118 — *2) Does data have a purpose?*
Page 126 — *3) Wisdom is nothing more than new data*

Chapter 8   Data; choice, decisions and railroading
Page 136   *1) Data for better decisions - nature or nurture?*
Page 148   *2) Data framing affects your perception of everything*
Page 162   *3) Is the data presented to us enabling a real choice?*

Chapter 9   Quantum Risk; A wicked problem that emerges at the
Page 176   boundaries of our data dependency
                 How does this effect data-based decision making?

Chapter 10   Peak Paradox
Page 192   *Exploring big issues without creating conflict*

ix   References *(Page 203)*

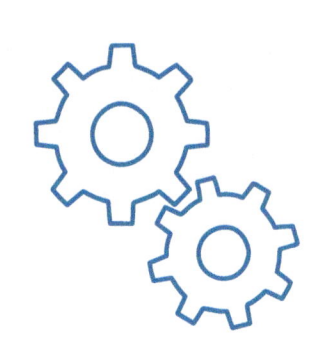

Chapter 1

Choice, decision making and judgement

Is your relationship constructive or destructive?

This chapter explains the relationship between choices, decisions and judgement, and how our questions indicate if our relationship is curious and constructive, OR linear, framed, and destructive.

This chapter is not another source of self-help, or an instruction to "use this framework to improve your decision making". It is for the curious, and those who ask questions on their journey.

Why is this an important topic?

Our individual and unique view of the world comprises layers of constructs created by our personality, biases, preferences, facts, and ideas, all learnt from past experiences. These constructs are better known as "mental models", which frame how we individually make sense of or align with the world. We continually develop sense-making frameworks, models, and maps in our brains that frame our perception of reality, thus affecting our behaviour and, consequently, our Choices, Decisions, and Judgements (CDJ).

Whilst we may not like it, our mental model frames how we see the world. I love how in this article[1], Cassie Kozyrkov[2] (chief decision-maker at Google) explains how to use the toss of a coin to determine how you see the world. Statistics predict one aspect of chance, but cannot predict how you will perceive the results when the coin has landed, and the outcome is not yet known to you. My dad taught me to toss the coins a few more times, until I got the result I wanted. It was a reinforcement model, teaching me that I had made the right decision from the possible two choices. On this topic, I would also suggest following and reading Lisa Feldman Barrett's[3] work, especially her new book "Seven and a Half Lessons About the Brain[4]". In this book, she explains that everything we perceive as reality is, in fact, constructed from fragments; ultimately, we have no idea what true reality really is *(yes, this is reinforcement bias - I am using quotes to frame your thinking, to align with my CDJ model)*.

In our digital era, new uncertainties, quantum risk[5], and increasing ambiguity constantly challenge our mental models[6] and how we accommodate and make sense of the world. The volume of noise and signals[7] coming into our brains is high, but we filter and convert it all into something that has meaning to each of us, according to our own unique mental model. We all inevitably reach different interpretations about what is happening, which can create frustration, confusion and misalignment. To remedy this, we can use questions to clarify and check our understanding and assumptions, and the quality of information provided. Slight differences may remain; and that which is unsaid, misled, guided, incentivised, or delivered with overconfidence, unfortunately, takes us from misalignments which are simple to remedy, towards tension, conflict and entrenchment.

This topic matters as directors are mandated to make decisions, but find that we are operating with misalignments, tensions, compromises, and outright conflict. This happens as the individuals sitting at the same table have agency[8] (along with their own mental models and incentives). We cannot be sure if we have made the right choices, or that we understand the unintended consequences or long-term impact of our judgements, until we talk about it.

Directors should unpack our relationship with choice, decision and judgement, as mental models, hierarchy and rules constrain us. This article is not about "how to ask better questions", nor does it suggest which questions you should ask (as some we don't want the answer to), but **how to determine if you, your team or your company has a constructive or destructive relationship with CDJ.**

When talking about CDJ in 2021, you would imagine that starting from the definitions should help. Unfortunately, it does not, as there is a recursive loop at play, with one definition requiring clarification of the other words, which themselves require the original definition. Amazingly, there are professional bodies for [decision making](#)[9] and [judgement](#)[10]; alas, even these cannot agree on how to define or clearly demarcate between intent and actions.

Our root problem is that everything, when framed with a maths or data mind, is a decision. When framed by a psychologist or social scientist, everything becomes a choice. To someone who has authority and responsibility, or plays with complexity, everything is a judgement. Confusingly, everything is an opinion to a judge!

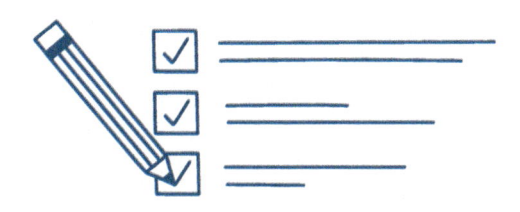

> Our root problem is that everything, when framed with a maths or data mind, is a decision. When framed by a psychologist or social scientist, everything becomes a choice. To someone who has authority and responsibility, or plays with complexity, everything is a judgement. Confusingly, everything is an opinion to a judge!

Here are the definitions from the Collins and Oxford dictionaries:

Choice

Choice [Countable noun] If there is a choice of things, there are several of them, and you can choose the one you want. [Countable noun] Your choice is someone or something that you choose from a range of things (Collins[11]). OR [Countable noun] an act of choosing between two or more possibilities; something that you can choose. [Uncountable noun] the right to choose; the possibility of choosing (Oxford Dictionary[12]).

Decisions

Decisions [Countable noun] When you make a decision, you choose what should be done or which is the best of various possible actions. [Uncountable noun] Decision is the act of deciding something or the need to decide something (Collins[13]). OR [Countable noun] a choice or judgement that you make after thinking and talking about what is the best thing to do [Uncountable noun] the process of deciding something (Oxford Dictionary[14]).

Judgement

Judgement [Uncountable noun] is the ability to make sensible guesses about a situation or sensible decisions about what to do. [Variable noun] A judgement is an opinion that you have or express after thinking carefully about something (Collins[15]). OR [uncountable noun] the ability to make sensible decisions after carefully considering the best thing to do. [Countable, uncountable noun] an opinion that you form about something after thinking about it carefully; the act of making this opinion known to others (Oxford Dictionary[16]).

Therefore, a **judgement** is the ability to make a sensible **decision** about a **choice**, which requires judgement about which choices to pick. As Yoda would say, "wise decision you make, stupid choices your judgement however selected."

The timeless challenges of Choices, Decisions and Judgment (CDJ)

"I change my mind as the data changes" is a modern digital age sentiment from the economist John Maynard Keynes, who is supposedly quoted to have said, "When the facts change, I change my mind." This sentiment likely arose from an early human bias, whereby leaders in war and battles refused to change their mind, even when the facts were in, and they had been proven wrong.

Choices, decisions and judgements are not difficult to make if you relinquish your values and ethics, blindly follow the incentives, or do not fully appreciate the impact of your actions. Still, we know that life is just not that simple.

Whilst we have created heuristics to remove choices, we have sought new ways to find data and facts to become evermore informed. But without making a choice, decision or judgement, we have no way of knowing if the new data is helpful or not.

The diagram here represents some of the timeless challenges of CDJ, which is a balancing act between what we know and don't know. It is our experience that enables the ghosts of the past to fight the voices of the present, as we try to decide what the spirits of the future hold, whilst being held accountable for the decisions we make today.

Figure 1: The timeless challenges of choices, decisions and judgement

Power and Control
"The ghost of the past"

— Whose policy, in what system?
— Incentives for what, and how did they occur?
— Constraints from agency and influence

Time and Consequences
"The spirit of the future"

— Whose rules apply tomorrow?
— Where will the pressure be?
— How far is the horizon, for each of us?

Questions, Data and Facts
"The voice of the present"

— Experience to get the right xxx vs experience that biases against the right xxx at this time
— Balancing "never enough" and "far too much"
— Seeking the right tool, analysis and bias OR the right outcome

Complexity and Truth
"Who decides who gets to decide?"

— Impact, but on what scale?
— How do I know what is true?
— Risk for who?

The point here is that it is always possible to find a reason to act or not to act, and the timeless challenge remains: that there is no perfect choice, decision or judgement. However, over time, and because we have choices, we can make decisions that improve our judgement, and in turn, enable us to find and make better choices. This is a constructive relationship between CDJ.

A destructive relationship would involve not liking the choices we face, procrastinating in the hope of a better choice occurring, and potentially losing a choice when the decision is made for you. In this instance, you won't improve your judgement and so you cannot determine if the next choice is any better - the impacts are cyclical.

Is the CDJ relationship about framing?

Looking back to the definition section at the beginning of this article, it is evident that there is a high degree of overlap and dependency between choice, decision making and judgement. As highlighted in the previous section, decision making can become complex very quickly, but our brain (mental models) demands patterns to make sense of it, and so we tend to come back to simple linear narratives which do not do our choices, decisions, or judgements justice.

What we have realised, but tend not to verbalise, is that none of our mental models or theoretical frameworks work in all cases, and indeed many established models of choice, decision making and judgement fail. This is why there is always a new book on the topic, with new self-help content that we have not seen before, allowing us to cling to a hope that the next model will work better - alas, it won't. I am aware of over 100 decision support models, and I suspect I have not really scratched the surface. An example below puts choices, decisions and judgements on a continuum between your own Northstar (choice) and that for a shared tribe, community or society Northstar. A linear model does not work at scale when dealing with complex environments, volatile situations, uncertain events, and ambiguous information. White flag time.

> What we have realised, but tend not to verbalise, is that none of our mental models or theoretical frameworks work in all cases, and indeed many established models of choice, decision making and judgement fail.

Figure 2: Choices, decisions and judgements

Choices	**Decisions**	**Judgements**
Biased towards a personal belief, your own Northstar, your mental model, your gut feel	Biased towards a group belief, a common purpose, a shared mental model, facts, data and analysis. Focus on reduction of risk	Biased towards a societal belief, common understanding, or a political policy. Focus on how to best compromise
Need for a personal North Star	Need for the leadership team to have a common Northstar	Need for a diverse team with a shared Northstar

#Lockdowns have enabled many social experiments. One such experiment has focused on consumer choice and buying behaviour. As we moved our food shopping online, and therefore missed the in-store sale specials, carefully placed sale items at the end of the aisle, large piled up offers in the entrance, and the sweets at the exit, our buying patterns changed as choice became more limited. We became creatures of habit, buying largely the same items, which reduced in variance over time. (This also highlighted that the UI and UX for shopping sucks). The option to shop in a more varied manner was taken away; so our choices decreased, although the variety was still there. So much for the Web creating perfect information, or the algorithm knowing exactly what you want.

As an alternative, we can determine that CDJ will change, depending on context and perception. The figure below highlights three examples, but what we can immediately conclude is that complexity in CDJ is generated by many variables, including the speed required, volume and quality of data, consequences of decisions, and the decision-maker's sense of enquiry, situation, and own mental models. Every known variable adds layers of complexity.

Figure 3: The different qualities of choices, decisions and judgements

The Size, Scale or Magnitude:

- **Choices**
  Deeply personal, including burden and impact

- **Decisions**
  Efficiency, effectivenes. Materially rewarded or incentive-driven

- **Judgement**
  Human-scale, doing the right thing, alignment and compromise

Frequency:

- **Choices**
  Seeking path known: Knowns always someone to ask

- **Decisions**
  Known: Unknowns have to action

- **Judgement**
  Unknown: Unknowns never enough data

Time and Urgency:

- **Choices**
  Limited to as few as possible

- **Decisions**
  Time-bound, shaped by urgency

- **Judgement**
  No deadline, continual review

Where are we up to, and where next?

So far, we have explored the relationship between choices, decisions and judgements. However, we tend to focus on the definition of decision making, rather than taking the time to understand if it is the right word to describe our actions. There is also no doubt that the word **decision** is preferable to the others, as it is perceived as more powerful and important than a choice or judgement.

The relationship between the three is causal, complex and relational, but we are educated and incentivised to adopt the simple linear view, and a single accompanying narrative. The reality is that judgement helps frame our choices, and making choices improves our judgement skills. Therefore, the relationship is not linear, it is circular. This circular relationship is enabled by the fact that we all have agency.

> The reality is that judgement helps frame our choices, and making choices improves our judgement skills.

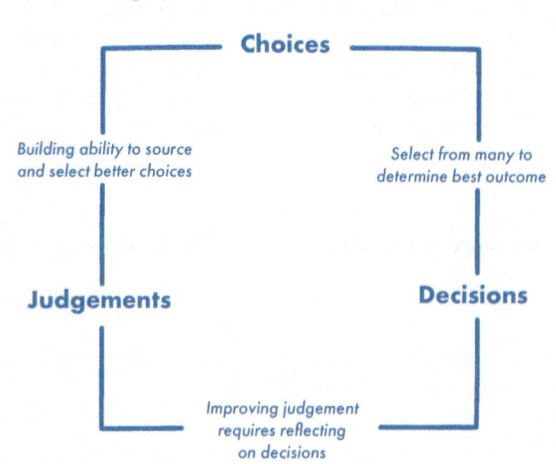

Figure 4: CDJ are interconnected

Choices

Building ability to source and select better choices

Select from many to determine best outcome

Judgements **Decisions**

Improving judgement requires reflecting on decisions

We know that the linear models are broken, as there is no universal tool to help with choice, decision and judgement. The next part of this book will explain the relationship we actually have between choices, decisions and judgement, and how our questions indicate if it is constructive and curious, OR linear, framed and destructive.

When thinking about CDJ, we tend to focus on the decision and choice axis. Indeed, if we can eliminate bad choices, we can improve decisions, but we ignore the fact that it is our judgement skills that help us to find the right choice. Procrastination is framed in our minds as a decision tool - time will remove choice and so a decision will become easier, either because a choice has been removed, or more data supports one option. On the contrary, more data does not make decision-making easier; nor does it guarantee that the decision made will be any better.

It is worth noting that academic work about "decision making" will always seek to create the most complex solution, because academics are incentivised to use the most advanced and new thinking (through publication, referencing, research and reputation pressures). Sometimes, simply tossing a coin is the perfect solution. The more we see the complex, the less we will accept the simple. In a linear world, in which we view choice, decision and judgement as a progression line - that we are given choices when young and make judgements when old and wise - we ignore continuous learning, and the need to exercise all three actions to become more proficient at decision making. Decision making is not a one-off task or a zero-sum end game.

As a thought experiment: if you had all the data[17] in the world, and adequate computing power to run a perfect forecast model, would you need to make further choices, decisions or judgements? To reach your view, I assume you have decided to either give every human full agency, or you have taken our individual agency[18] away. Now, in my definition of data, which might be different to yours, how we all behave with our agency is just data - which opens up a can of worms for each of us. Can we have full agency (freewill) and all scenarios be modelled? What do we mean about behavioural modelling, agency, data and, even more precisely, all data[19]?

Getting to one dataset, one tool, or one choice hides layers of complexity - which may enable one better decision, but is unlikely to be a long-term solution to improving choices, decisions and judgement. You have/ had choice, you make/ made decisions, you exercise/ exercised judgement. As discussed throughout this chapter, judgement supports you in finding choices.

How the questions we ask inform us!

The questions you are currently asking will help to inform where you are in the cycle, indeed, if you already have closed the loop and have a constructive cycle in place, or you are stuck in a linear, destructive relationship with choice, decisions and judgement.

The circular framing that I have used means that we will be asking different questions at every stage of the decision-making process.

Given that a board has to deal with many situations, all at different stages, in every meeting, we should see all these questions asked at every meeting, though framed to the specific agenda items. If there is no variation in the questions asked, surely it tells us something. Indeed, are we using our learning at each stage of the cycle to further improve the next outcome?

Figure 5: characteristics of CDJ

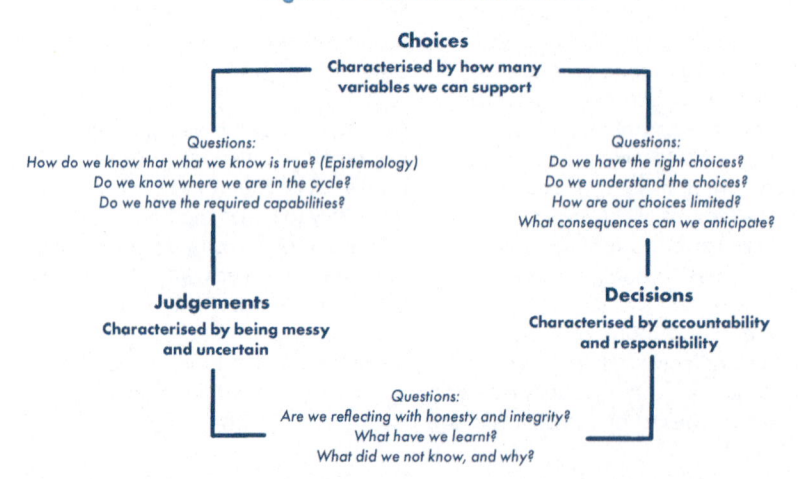

Choices
Characterised by how many variables we can support

Questions:
How do we know that what we know is true? (Epistemology)
Do we know where we are in the cycle?
Do we have the required capabilities?

Questions:
Do we have the right choices?
Do we understand the choices?
How are our choices limited?
What consequences can we anticipate?

Judgements
Characterised by being messy and uncertain

Decisions
Characterised by accountability and responsibility

Questions:
Are we reflecting with honesty and integrity?
What have we learnt?
What did we not know, and why?

The destructive "cycle" is not a circular, but a linear model, as it is fundamentally disconnected from the learning-based idea that uses choice and judgement to focus on better decision making. Instead, it relies on the assumption that by reading a new book or going on a new decision-making course, we will automatically get better at making decisions. To this model, iterative improvement requires an external influence.

This influence could be mentoring or coaching, and the mentor keeps you from closing the loop, either because they don't know how to, or it would not support their business model. Indeed, books, education and courses have no interest in you closing the loop, and instead will always make you believe in a new tool, method, or process - it is their business model!

Figure 6: CDJ for children, adults and seniors

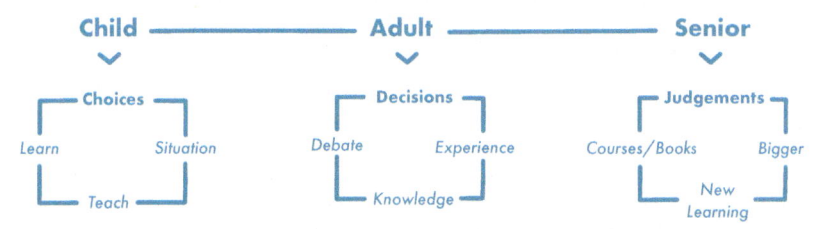

```
    Child ──────────── Adult ──────────── Senior
      ▽                   ▽                  ▽
  ┌─ Choices ─┐      ┌─ Decisions ─┐    ┌─ Judgements ─┐
Learn       Situation  Debate   Experience  Courses/Books   Bigger
  └─ Teach ──┘        └─ Knowledge ┘                New
                                              └── Learning ──┘
```

Instead of supporting these business models, we should reflect and question ourselves. In the boardroom, or in senior management meetings, is someone always asking the same questions? Does the agenda mean that as a team, individuals are unable to ask different questions? Or is it that others are influencing the agenda, keeping it framed to the decisions and outcomes they want? If the choice that those individuals want you to make is already the best supported case (other choices are railroaded[20]), why would they enable requests for more data? Do you have observers or assessors who look at the questions you ask as a team to determine if you are asking the right questions (something I am learning to do)?

Can the strength of the team's skills in choice, decision and judgement be determined by the questions asked in the meetings (something I am exploring)? A key question I often come back to when thinking about choice, decisions and judgement is "What are we optimising for?" In attempting to answer this, I find the model below a helpful guide. In a linear model, this diagram would present movement from a single choice in the lower left quadrant, to complex judgement in the top right. In a cyclic, learning model, choice, decision and judgement are of equal importance, however the lower left quadrant would be a more appropriate learning and experience-gaining context for mentoring, or succession planning, than the top right.

Figure 7: What are we optimising for?

	Complex: many externalilties	
Short Term: less than 3 years	Wider view, with more data and a model, but focused on delivering KPI, incentive or BSC for remuneration and bonus	Complex understanding of consequences and implications. Requires good dataset, and model that has scenario capability
	Narrow and framed. Most likely to be an opinion that proves to be wrong but delivers KPI, incentive or BSC for remuneration and bonus	Longer-term view, with more data and a limited model, but focussed on narrow outcomes and unlikely or unable to adapt to new information	**Long Term: more than 10 years**
	Simple: one externalilty	

Why does this matter? Because, right now we have increasing quantities of data, along with more vulnerabilities, ambiguity, complexity and uncertainty. The volume of moving variables (change) and the rate of change breaks the linear model, as we can never match this model with the complex situations we face. Therefore, there is a need to move from linear ideas of choices, decisions and judgement, to a circular way of thinking. Linear thinking is the best model when there are limited options and external stability. However, we now have many options, more variables, and increasing instability.

As [your company is owned by no-one](#)[21] (yes you read that right - a company owns itself. Follow the link if you need to read more on this), and a company cannot think for itself, we (the directors) must do the thinking for it. We are given, in law, the authority and responsibility to act on behalf of the company. This is "fiduciary duty". It is the reason that directors must move from a linear perspective on decision making, to a circular improvement and learning process, involving choice, decision making and judgement.

> One of my proposals to support better governance is to request that companies publish the questions asked in their board meetings. Not the answers, but definitely the questions.

Chapter 2

The shadowy hierarchy

I remain curious about how we can make better or wiser decisions. I am sharing this chapter as part of my own journey, as I unpack the mental boundaries and models that prevent me from making better decisions.

Context

Personally, I have, and will always, dislike and distrust "traditional" hierarchy, probably because within such structures, I perceived that the "power" wielded over me would never be available to me. I was always on the outside; one of the joys of neurodiversity is that you become aware, at an early age, of the need to align with the dominant system and structure. For me, there was no natural alignment. So, you either fight to fit in, fight the system, or create your own way of working. For many, fitting in is natural, but for me it never happened, and I stupidly opted for creating my own systems. I rebelled against the traditional system and structures in place, as I could only see hierarchy as a method of control to something I could not align with. To ask me to adhere would mean telling me to do things that made no sense - like writing with your right hand, as a lefty.

I am not alone; from Machiavelli to Second Lieutenant Boris Drubetskoy, in Tolstoy's War and Peace, many have realised that there are two structures of power. There is an obvious hierarchy of control, reporting, and subordination, and there is a second, unsaid and unwritten, hierarchy of lobby and access. The obvious structure is easy to rebel against. The lobby and access inner ring is where true power rests; it is the one to try and join. However, membership is by invitation only, and many will sacrifice more than they realise in terms of ethics, morals and beliefs to sit, and remain, at the table. When thinking about data, bias and decision making, the incentive to join and remain in the club is a critically important driver.

This unsaid shadowy hierarchy creates outcomes that we did not plan for, as some will jeopardise judgement and trust to be rewarded in the shadowy hierarchy. I could not align to this hierarchy either, as it was evident to me that you can only become a partner in a big firm when you have a big mortgage, which depends on a big salary. This significant debt and dependence on salary provide leverage. The humour in "[Yes Minister](#)[22]", the 1980's BBC political satire sitcom, exposed much of this way of thinking.

Why does this matter? We increasingly talk of equality and diversity (race, gender and neuro) agendas at the board, and in the senior leadership team, but it is increasingly evident that there is a hidden inner circle influencing the business, which means we are not making smarter or better decisions. The targets for transparency and equality are just that, targets (says the white, over 50 years old, male!).

I appreciate that it is difficult to separate the two dependent and co-joined aspects of the hierarchies. **One aspect represents power and control**, which is realised in terms of budget, size, scope, authority, and political dominance. **The second shapes how and where important decisions sit. Unfortunately, those who lobby may be unable to access the insights that data now provides to enable complex decision making.**

These separate but parallel structures have successfully coexisted for a long time, as the consequences of long-term decisions and intergenerational outcomes were not rewarded or measured.

However, Environmental, Social and Governance (ESG), the climate crisis and the brutality of our assault on our environment, coupled with data, means this is all changing. Despite this, those who gave everything to join the inner circle have an incentive to maintain the status quo for as long as possible.

> **What ghosts exist in the system, that mean our best-intended decisions do not create the outcomes we desire?**

Take a moment to reflect. In your experience, are there separate hierarchies in existence, or are they the same thing? Today, it matters more than ever before, as we now have to make long-term decisions against the backdrop of these systems of short-term incentives and rewards. The inner ring becomes blind to a hierarchical structure that always gives the feel of power - their short-term decisions continue to be highly rewarded through immediate incentives, and being in the club remains valuable for the few.

This viewpoint looks at these two hierarchies (formal and informal) but does not position one in the shadow of the other. Why am I analysing both - because we appear to find short-term incentive-driven decisions easy but struggle to make long-term judgement. I do not doubt the integrity of leaders who want to make better, data-driven long-term decisions, and be better ancestors, but get frustrated that it does not work. This is because there are likely ghosts from the old decision-making and lobby hierarchy in our current processes, creating outcomes that were not planned.

Note: The concept of a Shadowy Hierarchy was extended from the original term "Shadow Hierarchy", which is used in management textbooks to describe the difference between a formal, published and public structure, and the one that actually has power in decision-making. Googling "The Shadow of Hierarchy" will lead you to the 2008 paper from Adrianne Heuritier and Dirk Lehmkuhl, which was part of an EU funded project looking at "new models of governance"[23].

Our past is not easy to face up to

There appears to be a much longer story that starts when decisions, power and control were more united. Over the past 5000 years, we have become increasingly short-term focused and as a consequence, we have separated the decision-making process for the long term from structures of power and control. There is no doubt that the structure of economics, along with other biases, contribute to the science of management incentive and short-term goals that drives this separation. However, the data technology that we have created is based on complex existing relational dependencies, which means signals that should become noise through the layers of analysis, in fact, become significant distracting "interruptions" at the board. When the traditional and shadowy hierarchy coexisted, noise and signals were hidden by the informal lobby, preventing more thoughtful long-term decision making based on data. Today, signals and noise instead create paralysis at all levels in business structures, as everyone has access to the data.

Should the head of a religious movement be leading planning for the next 100 years, or ensuring this quarter's budget is spent according to the plan? Should our political leaders respond to the daily news headlines, or ensure we are equipped to face a global pandemic? Should the head of state be allowed to focus on sustainability, climate, and other global concerns, or defending their grandchildren's choices? In a joined-up power and decision hierarchy structure a long time ago, a few individuals could make those decisions and choices, and lobbying worked. Today, our hierarchies, like our decision making, have become paralysed, confused and ineffective, as the volume of data and signals mixed with noise has risen to a level that breaks our ability to know the right thing to do.. Currently, we have not transitioned to something that works. Indeed, lobbying has also failed, as it has become increasingly linked to short-term rewards and incentives.

The figure below captures this concept on a two-axis chart of scale and impact. The bottom right being just an idea, it has no scale and little impact. In the top right is big government, global businesses, global NGOs and charities, global religions and other large-scale movements. On the journey from the idea to the global scale, we either transition from our ability to make long-term decisions, shifting our focus onto quarter-by-quarter reporting, and justifying the delta between actual and plan, *or* we pay attention to intergenerational consequences. Risk, funding, capital and markets have a significant impact on the loss of that long-term thinking, as the rewards for the players in these arenas become aligned to short-term incentives. Whilst the long-term hierarchies become corrupted, the shadowy hierarchy of lobby gives way to a different incentive and power game. Impact and scale create the same problems irrespective of the organisation; short-termism can be recognised and rewarded.

Figure 1: Making better decisions

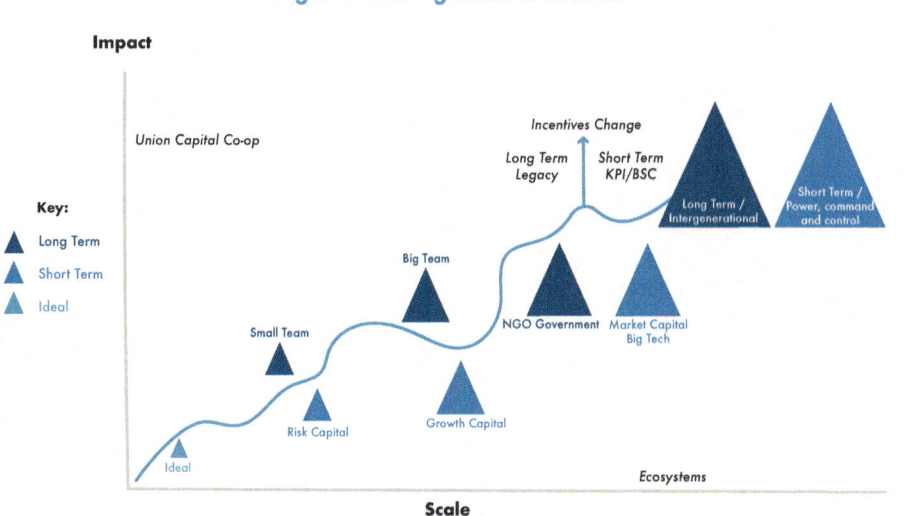

Impact

Union Capital Co-op

Incentives Change
Long Term Legacy | Short Term KPI/BSC

Long Term / Intergenerational

Short Term / Power, command and control

Key:
- Long Term
- Short Term
- Ideal

Big Team

Small Team

NGO Government | Market Capital Big Tech

Risk Capital

Growth Capital

Ideal

Scale — Ecosystems

Complex	**Complicated**
Enabling constrained (loosely coupled)	Governing Constraints (tightly coupled)
Probe - sense - respond	Sense - analyse - respond
Emergent Practice	Good Practice
Chaotic	**Obvious**
Lacking constraint (de-coupled)	Tightly constrained (no degress of freedom)
Act - sense - respond	Sense - categorise - respond
Novel Practice	Best Practice

Joseph, as in the Bible story and multicoloured dream coat fame (aka the Tim Rice and Andrew Lloyd Webber musical). It is one of the earliest written examples of man's capability for longer-term planning. It was a 14-year cycle, so not long term, but including 7 years of abundance followed by 7 years of famine. A cycle of growing, harvesting, storing and distributing. 4,000 years on, and a 14-year strategic planning cycle looks massive, but still short compared to the famed 100-years-plus Chinese and Japanese plans. I may have rose-tinted glasses in my view that we were once better at long-range forecasting, and alternatively, this piece from three world-leading experts asks "is humanity, in fact, unable to successfully plan for the long-term future?[24]". In the context of our currently limiting systems - yes. We have to break the system. I smell revolution.

Complexity of relationships

No doubt, a small part of the issue with our inability to long-range plan is the management of the complexity in our relationships. The web of collaborative relationships that we need to consider only ever becomes more strained, detailed, involved, dependent, and unbalanced, as each party aligns with their respective incentives and rewards. Critically, the unbalanced nature of relationships means it is increasingly difficult to predict outcomes and reactions (search: emergent complex systems). The commercial framing of relationships is explored in the figure below.

Figure 2: Unpacking ecosystem relationships

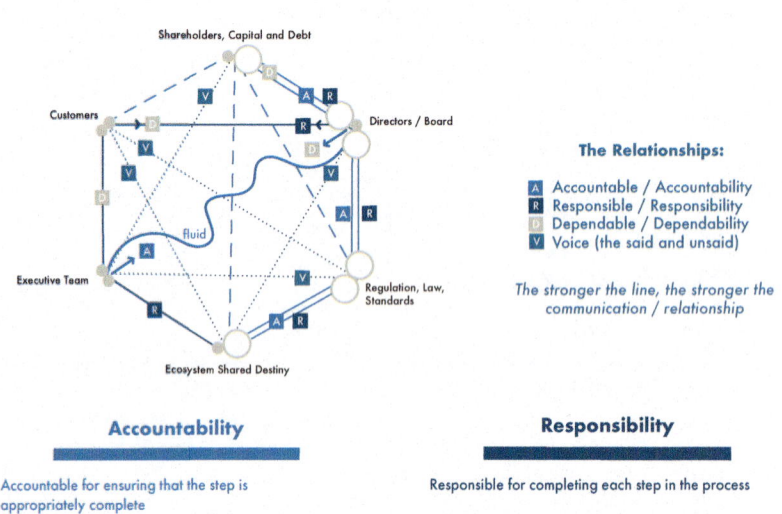

Nodes: Shareholders, Capital and Debt; Customers; Directors / Board; Executive Team; Regulation, Law, Standards; Ecosystem Shared Destiny

The Relationships:
- **A** Accountable / Accountability
- **R** Responsible / Responsibility
- **D** Dependable / Dependability
- **V** Voice (the said and unsaid)

The stronger the line, the stronger the communication / relationship

Accountability

Accountable for ensuring that the step is appropriately complete

Only one person can be accountable for the action

"Where the buck stops"

Responsible for ensuring that the work, task or process is completed to the required standard

Make the final decision about the work, including YES or NO authority plus veto power

Has ultimate ownership of the activity

Liable for any faults

The person accountable to see that work gets done

Accountable sign-off or approves the work 'responsible' provides

Set rules and policy

Directs, validates and approves

Responsibility

Responsible for completing each step in the process

Many people can be responsible for one action

The "doer"

Responsible to the person accountable

Assigned to do the work

Works on the activity

Entrusted with the task

The person responsible for doing the work

Delivers on 'accountable' person's brief

Develops and makes happen

Facilitates, coordinates and clarifies

The shareholder has a dependency on the board to make a decision that supports their funding of the capital. In contrast, the directors are accountable and responsible for their decisions, including unlimited liability. Everyone now has a voice that can affect choices and actions. The Director/ regulator/ ecosystem axis is dominated by those with the accountability and responsibilities, which are different for each stakeholder in an ecosystem, and are often driving in different directions because of Balanced Scorecards (BSC), KPIs, incentives and "being in the club". OKR (Objectives and Key Results) are no better, and the difference between build vs operate is a false one for the long term. Building the wrong thing can be very well rewarded in OKR land.

Continuing with the model, there is a remarkably fluid relationship between the executive team and the board, where the board depends on the exec team. Still, the exec team is accountable to the board (The level of fluidity varies by national and company law.) In this respect, the relationships between and with the customer are particularly misunderstood, but ultimately, the law says that the directors are held accountable. Each of the roles in this chain of visible, accountable relationships, from shareholders to the executive team, requires individuals capable of dealing with complex judgement.

However, the informal shadowy hierarchy remains unseen, posing problems to accountability and influencing the formal power structures within the business. *Let's expand:*

> **We face three connected, but not mutually exclusive, issues because they are part of an ecosystem.**
>
> 1. Some individuals in positions of influence and power are part of the "club", or want to be in the club, and therefore have incentives to do so. Their judgement and actions are aligned with those incentives.
>
> 2. Some individuals have achieved influence and power, but cannot grasp new mental models and skills to enable complex judgement. Their judgement and actions are aligned with their experience.
>
> 3. Some individuals can understand complexity and seek to explain and justify decisions and actions in this way.

Figure 3: Plotting individuals' skills/abilities in varying levels of decision environment complexity

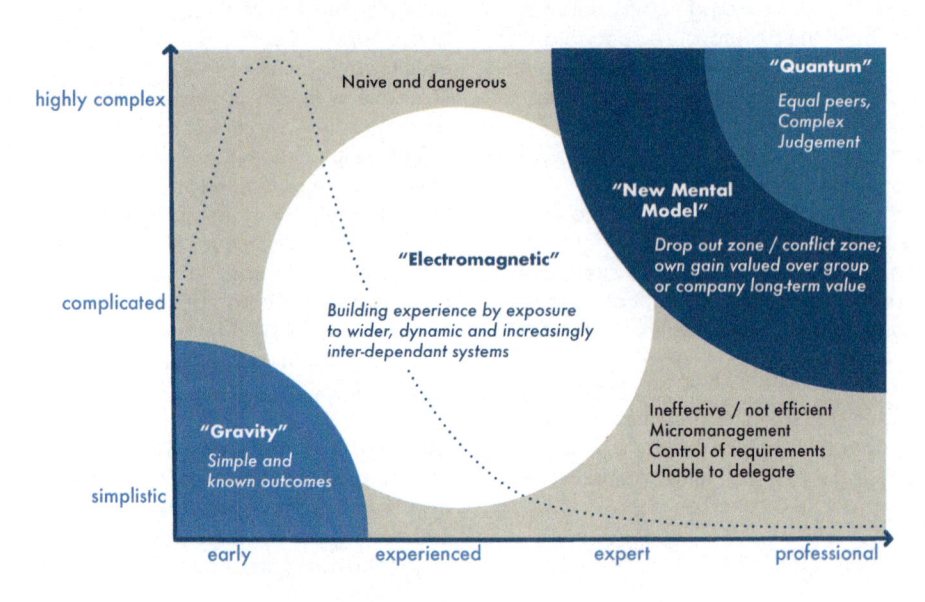

Y-axis: highly complex / complicated / simplistic
X-axis: Skill, ability and expertise level — early / experienced / expert / professional

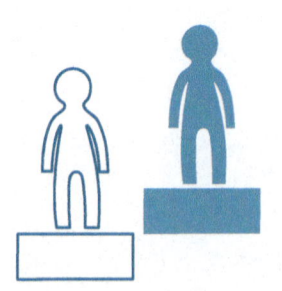

- Naive and dangerous
- **"Quantum"** — Equal peers, Complex Judgement
- **"New Mental Model"** — Drop out zone / conflict zone; own gain valued over group or company long-term value
- **"Electromagnetic"** — Building experience by exposure to wider, dynamic and increasingly inter-dependant systems
- **"Gravity"** — Simple and known outcomes
- Ineffective / not efficient; Micromanagement; Control of requirements; Unable to delegate

☐ ■ ■ ■ = Models   ■ = Result of Circumstance   ········ = How many are capable?

The diagram above shows a decreasing number of skilled individuals who can cope with increasing complexity. This is because the mainstream training system focuses on effectiveness and efficiency, and not on determining if you are doing the appropriate thing (efficacy).

Many arrive at senior roles and find they have to shift their mindsets; some do, and some don't, but they both now have decision-making power.

For example, we know that systems that create inequality, insecurity, and unsustainable practices are not easily transformed. Think of our government and economy. We have a system where 95% of the world lives meal-to-meal, day-to-day, week-to-week or month-to-month. An additional 4.99% can survive for 6 to 8 months on their available cash and funds.

Less than 0.01% (80 Million) of the world's population can plan for more than a year. When you have those 0.01% in power and lobby, will they ever need to vote for change? On this topic, it is worth following and reading Umair Haque; I love this essay[25], "How the Economy is Designed to Keep You Poor and Powerless."

> The laws of 1%[26] explore outcomes if we change everything by + or - 1%, and what this means for human behaviours.

What do "ghosts in the system" look like?

Imagine you are at the fairground, and there is one of those stalls where you get to throw something to win a prize. In the UK, we have the Coconut Shy[27]. You pay to get three balls or bags, stand behind the line, and throw them one at a time at your coconut of choice. Knock a coconut off, and you win it - a simple game of skill (apparently). However, when there is a ghost in the system, it is not so simple. You line up your ball on coconut number one (it is the biggest one) and throw it with all your skill.

As the ball approaches, the coconut moves and your ball sails past. You line up ball 2, aiming again at the largest coconut (the biggest prize); this time, you miss, but coconut number 4 wobbles - your last chance on this budget.

Lining up coconut number one for the last time, you hit it, but it does not fall off - coconut number 6 does, the smallest one. The ghosts win. Your desired outcome was coconut number 1; you got number 6. It was not your lack of skill - coconut number 1 is glued on. Different motivations and rewards were at play.

The ghosts make signals and noise

This chapter started by focusing on hierarchy, and I want to return to thinking about the two hierarchies, one of decision and one of power, and unpack the issues that an abundance of data has created for us. The diagram below sits with the idea that there is a natural order of decision making and power.

The movement from the bottom to the peak is a move in the decision-making time horizon. Overlaid on this model is VUCA (volatile, uncertain, complex and ambiguous)[28] situations. VUCA came from preparing/ training the soldier who would have to face a decision-making situation.

Figure 4: VUCA as situational decision making

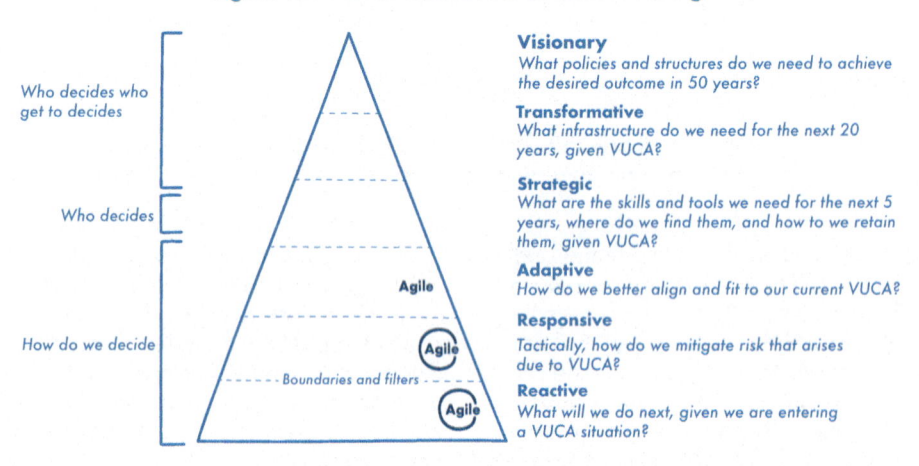

Who decides who get to decides

Who decides

How do we decide

Boundaries and filters

Visionary
What policies and structures do we need to achieve the desired outcome in 50 years?

Transformative
What infrastructure do we need for the next 20 years, given VUCA?

Strategic
What are the skills and tools we need for the next 5 years, where do we find them, and how to we retain them, given VUCA?

Adaptive
How do we better align and fit to our current VUCA?

Responsive
Tactically, how do we mitigate risk that arises due to VUCA?

Reactive
What will we do next, given we are entering a VUCA situation?

The hierarchy is worth a paragraph to unpack, as the context of VUCA is situational. Frontline workers are trained to be reactive. They know how to act based not on scenarios, but on the situation (police, army, emergency, fire, medical, call centre, customer-facing representatives). How they react is a matter of rules and heuristics, and is repeated numerous times in their training. As the NIKE brand says - "just do it". This becomes easy when you have trained to do the same thing for 10,000 hours - you don't have to think; it is an immediate reaction. Above this line, in the "responsive" tier, are the supervisors or team leaders, who ensure that the environment the workers operate in exposes the lowest possible risk. Above this, in the "adaptive" layer is management, who considers how to adapt to new situations and threats. Above them is the "strategic" layer, who asks "what skills do we need for the next five years, where are the skills gaps, and how do we access those skills?".

For most companies, this takes us to the CEO. However, in public operations, there are two more layers. The transformational layer is thinking about the infrastructure for the next twenty years, and finally, we come to the policymakers. The policy leadership team should be thinking 50 years ahead, considering what policy we will need to form, and how. Even with this simple layering, we can see that global leaders – from presidents, prime ministers, and heads of state – struggle to plan for 5 years ahead, yet are tasked with 50. We are not 10 times better for doing so; we have created a system 10 times worse.

What we should be witnessing here is that one layer's signal is another layer's noise. Each layer takes all the signals from below – this becomes their noise – and detects new signals that they then work towards. An upward flow – not a downward instruction.

As the figure below shows, each layer must apply different skills to find the signals needed to do their role. Interestingly, the lowest layers have the most operations discretion, as they are exposed to the highest operational risks. Most diversity is welcome, but not from those who cannot do the same action in every situation. Innovation may not be your friend in the depths of delivery. Meanwhile, the strategy layer has peak decision discretion. Innovation is critical, and so here, all diversity is critical. At the pinnacle of this hierarchy is policy discretion, where the least personal risk exists and where diversity is essential, but so is adherence to a Northstar and single vision – so less diversity might help. Diversity is about situational improvement in decision making for better outcomes. Ouch.

Figure 5: Finding the signals

1. Peak policy discretion, values and principles lead, least exposed to risk. Max diversity in all areas, including race, gender, neuro

2. Peak decision discretion, performance and incentives lead, mitigating/managing risk. Diversity in race and gender. Some consider diversity healthy for decisions but might instead focus on coherence

3. Peak operational discretion, rules and compliance lead, most exposed to physical risk. All think the same. Diversity in race and gender, but not cognitive, which is critical at the top

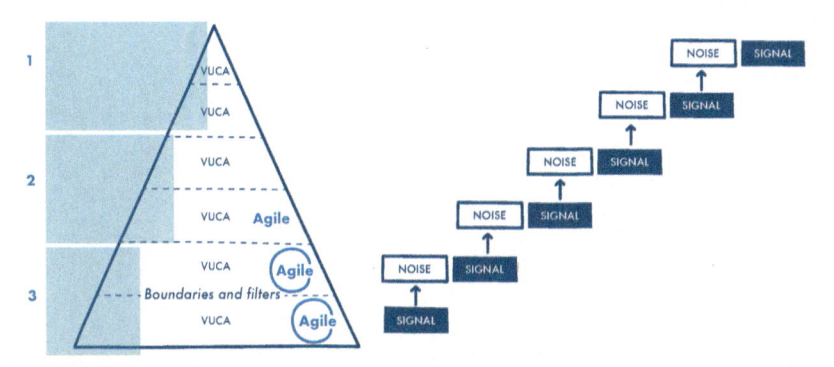

49

However, this is not what we are witnessing right now - the diagram above is theoretical rubbish. What we are truly feeling is summed up in the diagram below. There are signals from the bottom, creating signals at the top - each layer adds more signals and noise. VUCA has gone from being applied to situational layers, to the entire organisation, where everyone is reacting to everything.

The ghosts of old processes and previous decisions are no longer limited to a single layer, as everyone owns everything, and must react to and understand situations. To repeat a previous line: today, our hierarchies, like our decision making, have become paralysed, confused and ineffective, as the volume of data and signals mixed with noise has risen to a level that breaks our ability to know the right thing to do. Currently, we have not transitioned to something that works.

Figure 6: VUCA in a power and control hierarchy

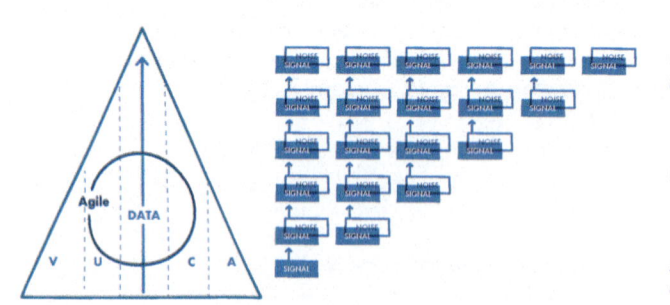

No whole ecosystem or collective policy, as no overall body

Incentives lead

Zero decision making, process and rules win

The observations in this diagram took time to collate, but the immediate question for us all is, do we believe what it presents, and if so, what can we do about it? Do you believe the challenges it presents should be considered within the context of "being in the club" and the resulting necessary compromises? Our millennials are not in the club and will not compromise; just ask them.

Our stability has vanished and our tools have broken

Even to a casual observer, we live in turbulent times, which is seen through an increase in VUCA. The difficulty facing boards, who carry responsibility for their decisions, cannot be overstated. We have to deal with the ghosts of the past, the voices of the present and the spirits of the future.

The diagram below looks at some of the tensions and conflicts being faced, as we struggle to determine what we are optimising for. The two axes are **communication** (said and unsaid) and **status** (known and unknown). The unsaid is that which is not written or spoken, but assumed, often to avoid more conflict.

> We have to deal with the ghosts of the past, the voices of the present and the spirits of the future.

Top right (said and known) - this is the day-to-day operational aspects of the board's and senior leadership team's roles. There are two camps (supporter and action owner) at the board, with 10 people involved in decision making. The focus is on management, KPIs, BSC and reporting. Data has a known status, and everyone is able and capable of engagement in the necessary topics. We are married to this quadrant and incentivised to focus on it, as it is easy and pays the remuneration we require.. This quadrant has traditionally depended on stability, but with VUCA disrupting that, and the increasing volume of signal and noise, we have to spend all our time here, as that is all we have time for.

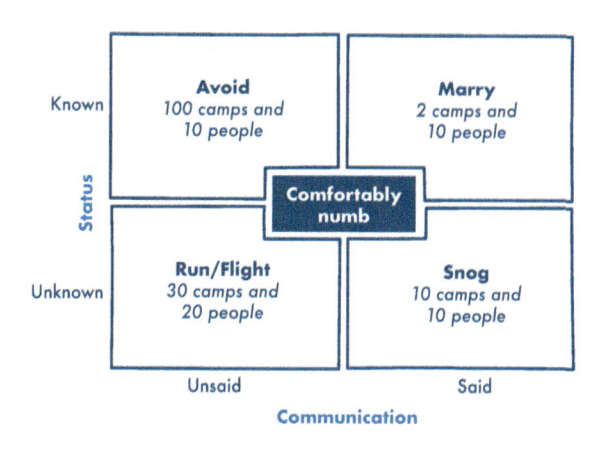

	Unsaid	**Said**
Known	Avoid — 100 camps and 10 people	Marry — 2 camps and 10 people
		Comfortably numb
Unknown	Run/Flight — 30 camps and 20 people	Snog — 10 camps and 10 people

Status / **Communication**

Note: Detailed diagram on following page

51

Figure 7: How camps and divisions change as we change status and explore communication

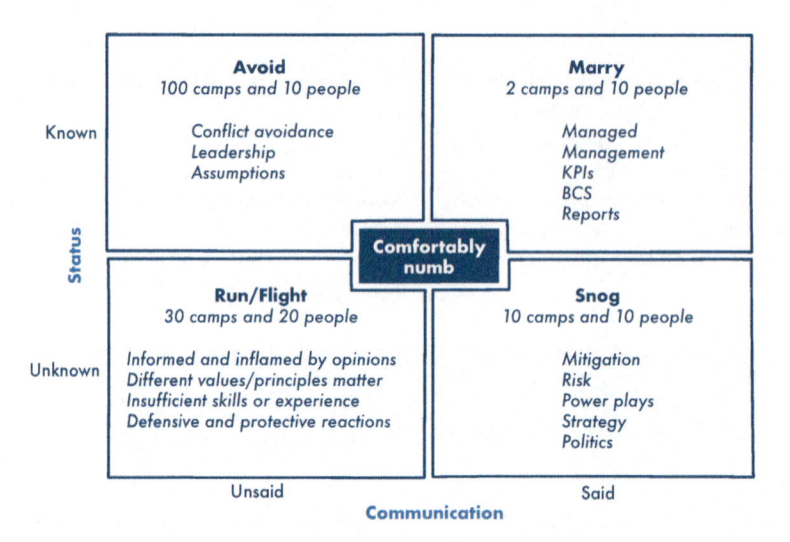

	Unsaid	Said
Known	**Avoid** 100 camps and 10 people Conflict avoidance Leadership Assumptions	**Marry** 2 camps and 10 people Managed Management KPIs BCS Reports
Unknown	**Run/Flight** 30 camps and 20 people Informed and inflamed by opinions Different values/principles matter Insufficient skills or experience Defensive and protective reactions	**Snog** 10 camps and 10 people Mitigation Risk Power plays Strategy Politics

Centre: **Comfortably numb**

Y-axis: Status | X-axis: Communication

The bottom right is both said and unknown. In these situations, everyone has a view on the unknown, resulting in 10 people in 10 separate camps (representing personal opinions and experiences). However, communication tends to be frank and honest. We go to this quadrant every now and again but quickly withdraw to safer grounds.

The known and unsaid is represented in the top left. The unsaid here includes the assumptions that we all make about everyone else in the room, and their viewpoints. This time there are 100 camps, as we all assume what everyone else thinks, and there is no communication. The principal reasons for poor communication are conflict, dominance and leadership style. We are trapped by the debt we have accrued (mortgage, credit, school fees, lifestyle, divorce) and need our salary; therefore, there is a need for control.

We try to avoid this quadrant, but every now and then, we end up there because of other stresses or pressures, the need for a diversion or to win a political game.

The bottom left quadrant shows the unknown and unsaid. The business ecosystem has a voice, the partners of the directors have a voice, everyone has a voice, and many of these players, due to previous flights and allegiances, are in several camps at the same time. The crux is that we are human and bring our differences, but because of this, situations can become very messy with what is unknown and unsaid. This quadrant represents the Volatility, Uncertainty, Complexity and Ambiguity (VUCA) we are currently facing, and that we don't have the tools to deal with it. Instead, we have a preference based on our skills, experience and incentives to focus on the top right quadrant.

Our processes and methods enable only certain decisions

One critical aspect of acting in a leadership capacity is to question and determine how our processes and methods guide and frame certain decisions. This means we have to unpack legacy and find the ghosts in the system.

> **Legacy within this framing is threefold. Decisions. Decisions. Decisions. These are:**
>
> 1. Previous incentives and power games created decisions, which themselves created processes, methods and rules; they are now ghosts in the systems. These decisions were taken so long ago that no one knows why, how or when it was decided. It is the way we do it; it is our IP, our brand.
>
> 2. Decisions that created "information and technology debt" include embedded and baked-in systems, hidden and no-longer supported code, and automation based on tools and data that was biased when originally created.
>
> 3. Decisions that created noise in the hierarchy, with the intention of losing or filtering signals that someone did not want to hear. This led to the creation of layers, reports, practices, structural regulations, and unchallenged assumptions.

Unpacking legacy questions will take time. It is worth asking questions about legacy when you are new to a company, and then verifying them over time, as we become blind to the tools that mould us.

I am focused on ghosts in the system because I want to determine how I can make smarter/ better decisions with data. For that, I need a data-decision framework. Therefore, I tend to ask what one thing - what do we, as a leadership team, want from our data?

The responses vary, but often include:

- Evidence-based, actionable insights

- What should we automate?

- How do we know we are doing the right thing?

- Where are there efficiencies to be gained?

- What do customers really want?

- How to manipulate customers to increase our margin and revenues?

- Where are risks that we cannot see?

- What is being hidden that we cannot see?

If you look at this list with the context of the tools and decisions that inevitably frame responses, consider - are these the questions that we are looking for data to answer, or are we instead looking for data to affirm/ justify that which we have already decided? A response that few would confess is "to justify what we are already doing!". This fits into the known/ unsaid quadrant in the previous matrix. The top left, the one we attempt to avoid opening up.

Data has bias because of previous decisions. Or we can write, "the ghosts of previous decisions will guide our present decisions". Importantly, our data, which we trust, is only the representation of the past, which means our current decision-making tools fail.

Therefore, as a leadership team, we have to find non data-driven tools to check which decisions from the past are influencing the current data, processes and tools in use. We cannot usefully answer the question we have set ourselves - "What is the one thing that we, as a team and organisation, want our data to drive, deliver or provide? - without understanding the situation.

The Chief Technology Officer (CTO) knows that the time has come to build a new platform when the bug list, new feature development and maintenance costs are bigger and more time-consuming than developing a new platform — this is the technology debt question. The Chief Information Officer (CIO) or newly created #CDO (Chief Digital Officer) role has to understand the business's information debt. The CTO will struggle, as there is no clear path from policy to code. Similarly, the CIO/CDO struggles with no clear path from policy (clear focus on one thing) to accruing better data for the complex decisions we are required to make. The data leadership team inherits, and is now accountable for, previous ghosts and decisions, which constrain what is now possible - the biased tool has created what we currently have. The costs of collecting, labelling, holding, sorting and creating training data continually increase, increasing the gap and misalignment in values and expectations from data.

"We become what we behold. We shape our tools, and then our tools shape us" is a quote often mistakenly attributed to Marshall McLuhan, and called McLuhan Law. The quote was actually written by Father John Culkin, SJ, a Professor of Communication at Fordham University in New York and friend of McLuhan. Such is the problem with data.

As we have new and different decisions, powers, and now data, perhaps we should reflect on these questions as a leadership team.

- What do we want to become, and which tools and data will help us?

- Which tools do we currently use, and where are they leading us?

- What is the minimum viable dataset required to deliver the most value?

- Do our current tools and data trap us?

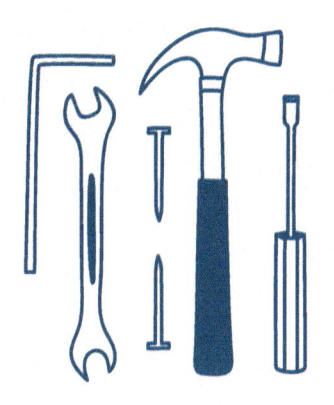

Is the work of data to "detect and measure" or to "enable change, and transform?"

Chapter 3

Are KPIs the nemesis of innovation?

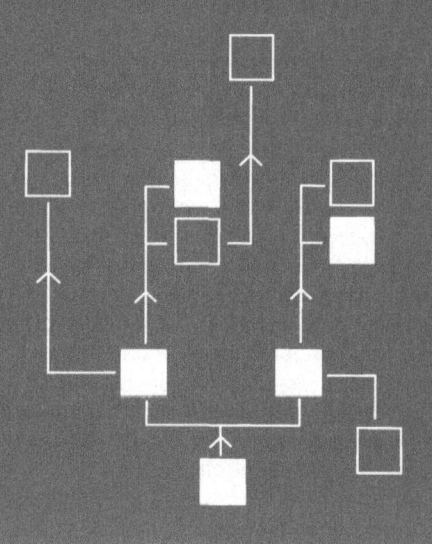

The focus of this chapter is on the application of data for growth through innovation. The insights are independent of company structure or leadership.

The prime recommendations are:

1. Discover and break the right number of critical links between outcomes and rewards/ incentives.

2. Find and modify reinforcement linkages between outcomes and culture so that all questions can be rewarded.

Unpacking the different systems & processes that control us in start-up & corporate lands

Apple's underlying philosophy is about being "better." It is likely that if Apple's executives were leading the response to COVID-19, they would not be planning for a "Return to Normal" or creating a "New Normal" - they would instead be focused on making what we already have, better!

In business today, the demands of complex judgement, coupled with evolving requirements in a volatile environment, mean that stability is prioritised over change. This is because risk is already difficult enough to explain and manage, without attempting to drive change. Outstanding leadership focuses on making one thing better - it must make a difference here, whilst attending to other concerns, for all-round better outcomes. Therefore, we must consider - what is the one stand-out priority that demands attention and focus, and has the potential to deliver "better"?

We should turn our attention to ensuring that the data provided for decision making has provenance and lineage, with the aim of improving decisions and achieving better outcomes. Therefore, the focus of this chapter is on the application of #data for #growth, through #innovation.

Central to the thinking in this chapter is looking at the linkages between measurement, performance, and management, and if outcomes can be improved as a result of these factors. The insights shared here are independent of company size, structure or leadership.

The prime recommendations are:

1. Discover and break the right number of critical links between outcomes and rewards/ incentives

2. Find and modify reinforcement linkages between outcomes and culture, so that all questions can be rewarded. The challenge in this chapter is choosing one thing to make better - as you will read, HR is a strong contender for this.

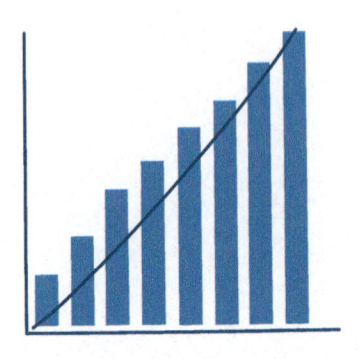

Figure 1 details the blocks that are used in each diagram that follows, which will describe the systems of innovation within business. The blue blocks are a choice or decision, the grey blocks represent drivers of people involved in the system, and the outlined block entails the beginning or end of a process.

Key:

Blue Blocks : Choice/Decision

Grey Blocks : People involved in the system

Outlined Blocks: Start or end of process

Figure 1: explaining the blocks

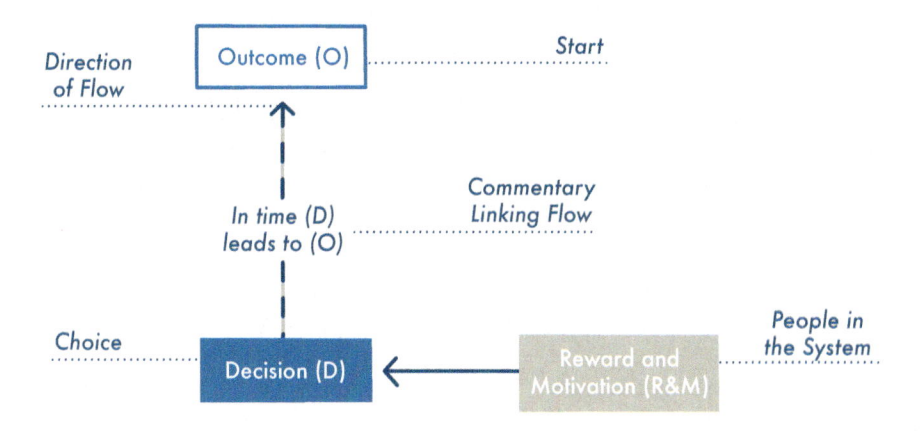

Direction of Flow

Outcome (O) .... Start

In time (D) leads to (O)

Commentary Linking Flow

Choice

Decision (D) ← Reward and Motivation (R&M)

People in the System

Figure 2 presents a generic & simplified innovation process in start-up land. The purpose is not to explain all innovation in all start-ups, but to identify critical differences between this and the corporate world, and why innovation feels easier here.

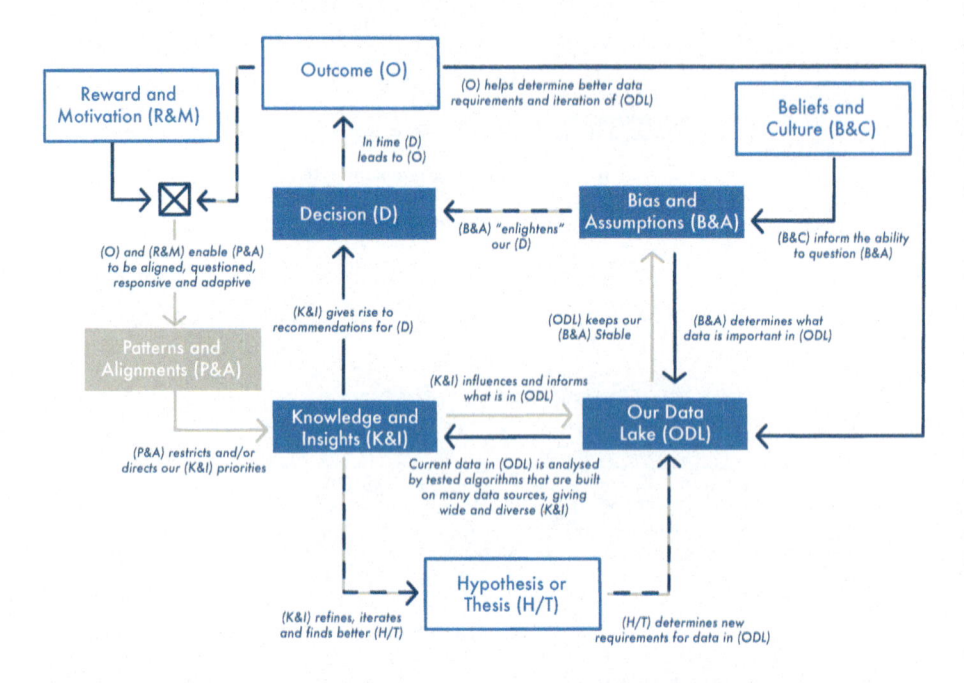

Figure 2: Innovation process in start-up land

Let's explain figure 2 - starting from the white block, positioned bottom middle of the diagram, "Hypothesis or Thesis".

Typically, a team will come together with an idea, and their "Hypothesis Or Thesis" determines the data required for "Our Data Lake". Then, there is a direct flow from a Data Lake[29] to "Knowledge and Insights", on the left. The decision-making process tests the Thesis that the team created, through analysis, using the available data. The analysis process generates Knowledge and Insights, which closes an agile feedback system as these refine what data we need in a Data Lake, to complement the analysis of this data, which tests the team's Thesis. Knowledge and Insights give rise to recommendations, which lead to "Decisions". Over time, Decisions become "Outcomes", which we measure. Knowing and measuring Outcomes help us to refine and better define the requirements we have for the data in Our Data Lake, thus creating a second, slower, iterative improvement system.

Our Data Lake has a relationship or correlation to the Bias and Assumptions we have as a team. This creates a closed-loop system between the two, that further helps inform the Data Lake, and reminds us of our Bias and Assumptions. A second influence on Bias and Assumptions is the team's Beliefs and Culture. Open cultures enable teams to question their Bias and Assumptions, whilst other cultures may avoid such questions. A culture that encourages questioning will enable open-minded teams to continually check if they have the correct Thesis and data in their Data Lake, and to undertake the analysis without creating an outcome that was forecast. Understanding the links between Our Data Lake and Bias and Assumptions helps us in our decision-making processes.

In a collaborative, open and free-thinking system, being able to check assumptions will enlighten decisions, leading to better outcomes. In an early-stage company, Reward and Motivation is not coupled to Outcomes, as there is no revenue generated, making direct causal correlation difficult to determine. The Reward and Motivation fundamentally relates to the team and individuals being driven to do their best. When it works well, the team is there to prove their Hypothesis or Thesis, and to grow a company based on their collective thinking.

Reward and Motivation structures also create Patterns and Alignments. When the team's perception of Patterns and Alignments is open, the loop is responsive and adaptive to questions and problems. We know our behaviours demonstrate the link between Patterns and Alignments, and the Knowledge and Insights we search for. We see this linkage in the methods and priorities that the team creates and focuses on. Priorities will give rise to recommendations, which lead to Decisions and Outcomes. These help us refine Our Data Lake to continually improve, and further hypothesise. An agile loop of continual improvement is created.

In start-ups, this system leads to rapid development and creative thinking within an adaptive, self-improving process. The continual improvement creates a refinement of hypotheses, data, and analysis, and is witnessed as better outcomes to create change. In a system driven by data, and containing the ability to challenge and question everything, we find that outcomes and culture focus on refining hypotheses, and the team continuously strives to refine and improve, supporting innovation and driving growth. In a positive agile loop, this feels easy, as the system enables flow.

> **Moving our attention to corporate-land, before the final recommendations are presented...**

Figure 3 presents a generic & simplified innovation cycle in corporate-land. The purpose is not to explain all innovation in all enterprises, but to identify critical differences to the start-up world, and why innovation feels more difficult here. What is immediately noticeable is that there are more dependencies.

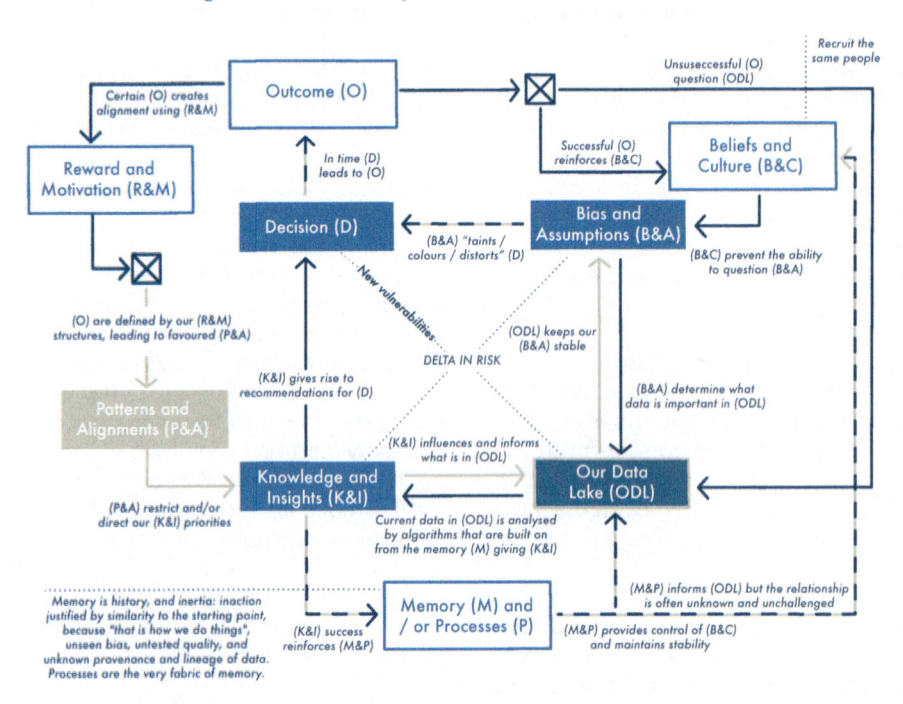

Figure 3: Innovation process in mature businesses

[Diagram showing the innovation process in mature businesses with the following key components and relationships:

- **Outcome (O)** — Certain (O) creates alignment using (R&M); Unsuccessful (O) question (ODL); Recruit the same people
- **Reward and Motivation (R&M)** — (O) are defined by our (R&M) structures, leading to favoured (P&A)
- **Decision (D)** — In time (D) leads to (O); (B&A) "taints / colours / distorts" (D)
- **Bias and Assumptions (B&A)** — Successful (O) reinforces (B&C); (ODL) keeps our (B&A) stable; (B&A) determine what data is important in (ODL)
- **Beliefs and Culture (B&C)** — (B&C) prevent the ability to question (B&A)
- **Patterns and Alignments (P&A)** — (P&A) restrict and/or direct our (K&I) priorities
- **Knowledge and Insights (K&I)** — (K&I) gives rise to recommendations for (D); (K&I) influences and informs what is in (ODL)
- **Our Data Lake (ODL)** — Current data in (ODL) is analysed by algorithms that are built on from the memory (M) giving (K&I)
- **Memory (M) and / or Processes (P)** — (K&I) success reinforces (M&P); (M&P) informs (ODL) but the relationship is often unknown and unchallenged; (M&P) provides control of (B&C) and maintains stability
- New vulnerabilities; DELTA IN RISK

Memory is history, and inertia: inaction justified by similarity to the starting point, because "that is how we do things", unseen bias, untested quality, and unknown provenance and lineage of data. Processes are the very fabric of memory.]

In figure 3, Let's start from the white block, positioned in the bottom middle of the diagram, which says "Memory and/ or Processes". This block was "Hypothesis or Thesis" in startup-land. Comparatively, in the corporate world, trading history has provided experience, teams, revenue and methodology; building memory and processes. These deliver barriers to entry, form IP, and often form the core value of the company.

A critical link is already established between Memory and/ or Processes and "Beliefs and Culture".

Often, this is visible in the recruitment of new employees who already adhere to the Beliefs and Culture of the company (to read more on this, search for [organisational fit](#)[30]). An influential culture determines the "way we do things" based on Memory and Processes, which usually removes the ability to question Bias and Assumptions ("this is how we do it" is taken for granted). We retain the same Bias and Assumptions which taints, colours or distorts our Decisions. Over time, Decisions become Outcomes. In mature businesses, all outcomes are measured *(what does not get measured cannot be managed)*.

We measure the success of our Outcomes. Successful Outcomes reinforce our confidence in our Beliefs and Culture - and that we should not change. Unsuccessful outcomes are seen as an error in the model, data or analysis, and the solution, that we need more of the correct data. The Outcome tends to favour or align to pre-established Rewards and Motivations, as incentives and bonuses are linked directly to Outcomes. With Outcomes measured, and aligned to Rewards and Motivations, we have a confirmation bias towards certain Patterns and Alignments, that favours individual success. These Patterns and Alignments restrict the options and learning from Outcomes and determine our priorities. As a result, we will search for certain Knowledge and Insights in our data set - especially ones that we can recommend as a Decision - to create an Outcome that aligns with our personal performance metrics, established by the Memory in the system.

In the centre of the diagram in Figure 3 is "Delta in Risk". This is an important point. When an organisation is finance-led, risk is modelled, defined and understood. Financial data and controls ensure that processes are designed to control risk, limiting to the agreed level. Data creates many dynamic changes within an organisation. Critically, data introduces clarity and an understanding of risks that could not be seen through the pure lens of finance. Ignoring cyber attacks and loss of data as a systemic risk, the data risk of particular interest here is the identification of new insights about products, services, teams, partners, and processes that data brings to the attention of employees and Directors - a delta in risk. Many of the closed-loop reinforcement and confirmation bias feedback loops can be identified, but are structured to ignore this new risk. Where risk is identified, it creates instability in memory, bias, assumptions and decision making. Still, because of the strength of existing processes, the tension may not lead to change but rather a higher level of frustration, denial and protectionism. Existing Processes have memory and efficiency of flow, and can incrementally improve that which already exists. The same memory that is designed to resist flow, is oriented towards a change of the process itself.

In a complicated closed-loop system driven by data, where Outcomes drive Rewards and Beliefs, and Culture removes the ability to challenge and question, our Memory and Processes continually reinforce the same Patterns. We find we are unable to adapt to the new vulnerabilities and risks that data brings, which is destabilising. We realise that our Processes are not set up to support disruptive innovation or iteration at scale. Data can define a set of possibilities and constraints, which may be located in Memory. Data is biassed and creates bias, and those biases are different and unique. Data has no imagination or creativity, and it will keep doing the same thing. Data cannot create a solution on its own.

Comparing the models

In mature businesses, innovation appears more difficult. My experience shows innovation itself is not more difficult, rather, the willingness to accept and create change, and adapt to and steer a new course that innovation brings, is constrained due to closed-loop feedback systems. The takeaway is that in start-up land there is less measurement of outcomes, meaning there are fewer linkages to confirmation bias loops. Are KPIs, the driver of measurement, therefore innovation's nemesis?

Figure 4 presents two different simplified innovation cycles - one in start-up land ("Early stage growth" and one in corporate-land ("Late stage efficiency"). The figure shows how closed-loop feedback systems arise in corporate-land, stifling innovation by focusing instead on efficiency and the measurement of outcomes through KPIs.

Figure 4: Simplified innovation cycles

Early Stage Growth

Outcome (O) → Our Data Lake (ODL) → Decision (D) → Outcome (O)
Hypothesis or Thesis (H/T) → Decision (D)
Beliefs and Culture (B&C)
Reward and Motivation (R&M)

Late Stage Efficiency

Outcome (O) → Beliefs and Culture (B&C) → Decision (D) → Outcome (O)
Finance and Budget (F&B) → Decision (D)
Memory (M) and / or Process (P)
Reward and Motivation (R&M)

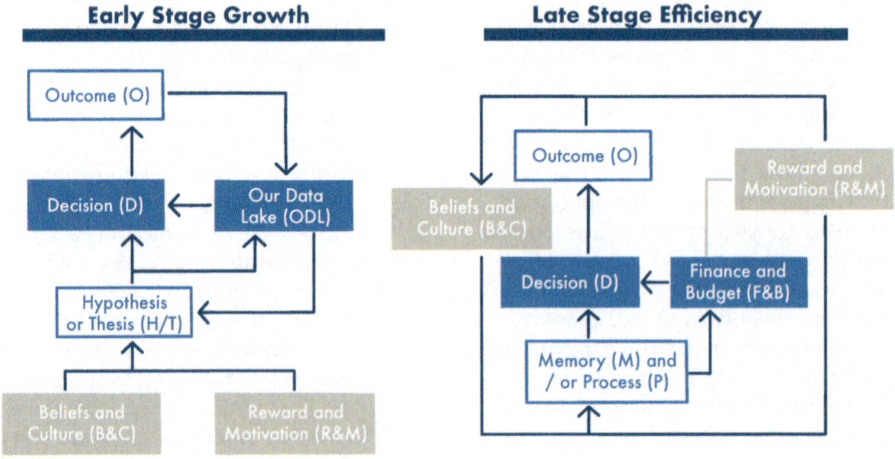

One example, from Mike Smith[31], describes three measurements that create continual frustration for innovation teams.

1. *"As a legal representative for this company, it's my job to make sure we don't sign any contracts that put us in a perilous position, and to make sure that we're abiding by all local laws and regulations".* This position states - I am a Fellow of my legal institution and am professionally bound by their code of conduct, and I am measured by how few lawsuits we are involved in, both with other companies and with other institutions. I am incentivised to avoid that risky innovative contract.

2. *"As the lead for HR in this company, and being responsible for employee retention and well-being, it's my responsibility to make sure we recruit carefully, following appropriate laws (no discrimination, etc.), and ideally minimise employee dismissals - as they are disruptive and represent risk to the company. "* In other words, I am measured on the avoidance of claims, and really don't want to recruit that brilliant and outspoken evangelist who has 1,000,000 followers on Black Lives Matter (BLM).

3. *"As CFO, I need to make sure our books balance and that we are fiscally responsible. When it comes to the product team needing money for research and development, we must balance investment with income, and ensure that the solvency of the company is not questionable."* This translates to - I am a member of a professional body and my reputation is my next job. It will count against me if, as the CFO, I agree to a large loan to accomplish some critical work that others view as essential for company growth, and it goes wrong. My bonus is based on avoiding risky financial transactions.

Often the system we have created for stability, measurement and risk avoidance, which rewards key individuals for doing their job well, can stand counter to innovation.

People in the loop

Whilst the innovation models recognise the processes that surround our peers, teams, people and staff, they do not wholly recognise the agency of individuals. Our company may have ethics but our divisions, functions and ecosystems all have their own unique moral codes, which change. Our company often thinks about one culture, rather than seeing 100 cultures, clustered by stakeholders and wider dependent communities, including extended family. The system, crafted for efficiency and stability, does not understand what is driving an individual at this moment, how they make a choice, and the implications of this choice. Humans are in the loop, but more often, are the loop. Humans are the workforces and feedback loops with their creativity, reluctance and behaviour-creating colour in a very greyscale, process-driven organisation. A simple model for innovation creation within business could become a 100 page book, just by including people's behaviour and attitudes as blocks at each node in the model.

Recommendations for breaking something to become more innovative!

My opinion, based on experience and experiments, is that innovation, disruption and transformation are difficult but not impossible. They all start from knowing what to transform. Therefore, if innovation is what you are seeking in mature businesses, here are some ideas:

- Find and break the right number of critical links between Outcomes and Rewards/ Motivations. This means taking a critical view of reward calculations, annual reviews, remuneration packages and incentive programs. HR will need to support this.

- Find and modify reinforcement linkages between Outcomes and Culture so that all questions can be asked and all questions are rewarded. This means that unsuccessful outcomes help to create more questions, and focus on remedy, not blame.

- Detach from a love of corporate memory to create a hypothesis, rather than a millstone.

- Find ways to enable and deliver the diversity of thinking that creates openness, focuses on values and behaviours more likely to result in a healthier culture, and may change the types of people you employ.

Chapter 4

Power, agency and influence: a new framework for complex relationships

In this chapter, I am going to explore the relationship between power, agency and influence. My intent here is to unpack each of these words and their relationships to one another. Power, agency and influence can interact in a constructive or destructive relationship cycle. In this chapter, we will explore how power, agency and influence, when in a constructive cycle, lead to better outcomes - and, conversely, how power, agency and influence in a destructive cycle lead to worse outcomes.

Developing a framework

As a society, we love the analogy of peeling an onion. We peel back one layer to reveal a new similar layer, each offering a new idea or thought, and adding complexity. Often, we use this model when analysing ourselves - to get to our inner core and understand our true values.

As we peel back each layer of power, agency and influence, we will find increasing complexity and interconnectedness; much of which we cannot grasp in the context of decision making and governance. As we peel back more layers of complex interconnections, we will find that there are more dependencies, which give rise to layers of uncertainty and ambiguity. Risk and uncertainty remain - no single outcome is guaranteed; there are always at least two possibilities.

We eventually find that we are not just peeling an onion, but unpicking different ideals and beliefs, with varying degrees of connectedness. Peeling the onion does not pick up the relationships and interconnectedness between the layers, it simply removes layers. Even when looking at different layers, we cannot necessarily see the dynamic and relational processes between different onions.

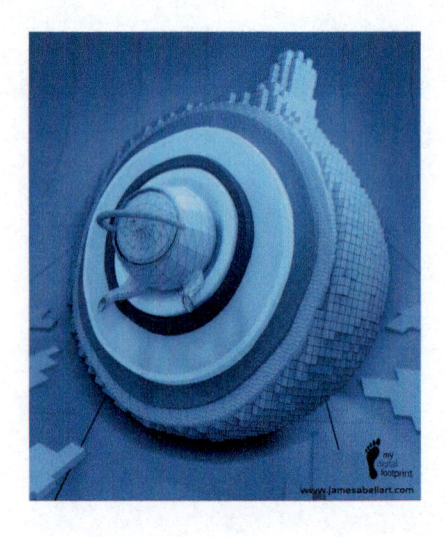

Power, agency and influence

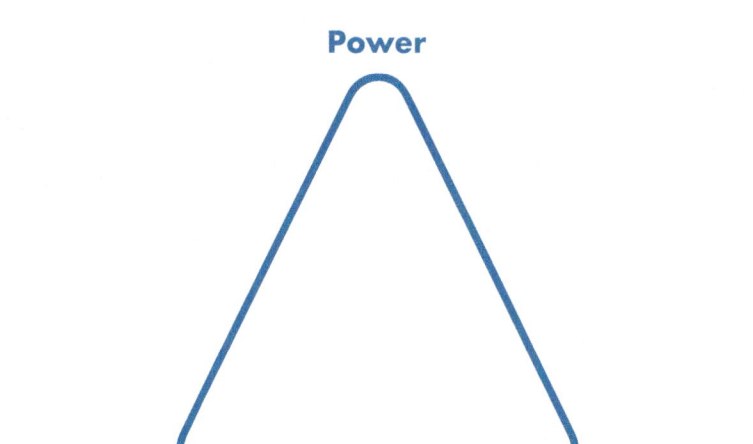

Figure 1: Power, Agency and Influence

```
           Power
            /\
           /  \
          /    \
         /      \
        /        \
       /_____\
   Agency        Influence
```

Power, in the context of figure 1, is realised when someone/ thing shows mastery and can exercise control. Control can be exercised physically/ by muscle, through the state (policy, legislation or law), through the mind, or via societal norms. There are enormous bodies of work which explore the vast and varying types of power. The purpose of this chapter is not to write an essay on power, but rather to understand power, in the context of agency and influence.

Here, we do not consider by whose authority power is sorted, taken or given, nor are we exploring the links to sovereignty - we only perceive that someone has control.

Agency in the context of figure 1, specifically human agency, can be defined as an actor who has the capacity to act. Individual agency is framed by our views on responsibility and accountability. Agency in relation to our actions depends on our motivations, capacity, and experience. Given that agency can be understood as an actor utilising their mental capacity, there is a deep link between agency, and biochemistry and nutrition. If we are to look at agency on its own or alongside concepts of traditional capacity, but without understanding the brain-gut axis, we won't fully appreciate why we might act in a certain way.

Influence, in the context of figure 1, is the actor, who in this case can help determine an outcome. The actor, as an influencer, can affect the character, development, or behaviour of someone or something. Influencers can use incentives, skills and tools on those with agency and power to achieve a desired outcome. Incentives may be economic - more power, more agency or money - and the influencer will have changed the behaviour of the system, players or actors, to have created the outcome that they wanted. To influence, they may use skills such as creating doubt, forgetting to pass on information, inducing guilt or shame, research, presentation of risk, or creating/ ignoring bias. The influencer who uses these kinds of skills is like Machiavelli - their desired outcome is achieved using any means. The tools that an influencer can use include: education, knowledge, facts, access, nudges, behavioural economics, and science.

With power, agency and influence, we have to consider who the actors are in each specific business context. In the vast majority of decision-making scenarios, the actor will come with a bias towards a political, economic/commerce or personal agenda. It is evident that when we discuss power, agency and influence, that power might rest with a politician, an actor with agency might be represented as a business, and an influencer could be individual. While many combinations are possible, this chapter will not explore all potential scenarios. Still, we will consider which forms of power, agency and influence lead to a constructive or destructive relationship, and how we might understand these situations. Looking at this will help us to inform the future of governance.

The scenario below begins with the influencer, who in this case, is the prime mover. It could also be entirely possible that we begin with the actor, with power or agency, as the prime mover. The scenario is summarised in Figure 2, *Destructive Relationships*.

Consider an influencer - in this case, a regulator - whose primary role is to construct and revise regulation. (*In many cases the regulator has power to enforce regulation, but consider that in this case, this power instead rests with those who provide the legislative framework for the regulator to exist, act and as such have teeth [powers]*). As an influencer of the market, you wish to have the most significant regulatory body possible. The larger the staff and reach of your regulatory body, the more kudos and job opportunities will reach the senior leadership team. You will win more awards[32] and be paid more.

As the influencer, you propose new rules, regulation and law to the person with power. It is important to note that power is always shifting in this relationship, as a regulator will alternate between delegating authority and taking on more power in order to create regulation. The relationship between the influencer and the person with power is such that the influencer persuades the power-holder that the more rules and regulations exist, the more power they will be able to accumulate. In this scenario, we can see that the power-holder is the government. The government, through its economic policy, believes that rules, regulations and laws provide the right degree of control and restriction over the people, who have agency.

The government's interpretation of what is best for the market leads them to believe that control and restriction will result in a more efficient and effective market than one left to run of its own accord. The people in business, with agency and possessing a free market position, now face a barrage of red tape, rules, regulations and laws in which they can operate. Those with agency treat the influencer with suspicion, and they are unwilling to share data or information openly. The influencer has to write more rules to ensure enforcement and adequate data reporting.

The relationship between the person with agency and the person with influence is one driven by secrecy and attempting to avoid the overly restrictive regulatory environment. This scenario creates a very destructive loop, one that we see in highly regulated markets. Each of the players is unable to break their behaviour. The influencer wants more rules and regulation, the power-holder enjoys the control and possibly a conflict of interest with tax income, and the person with agency finds every way to ensure there is not more regulation, by sharing the least information possible and adhering to tick-box compliance.

> What leads to relationships becoming destructive - as in, poor decisions and worse outcomes?

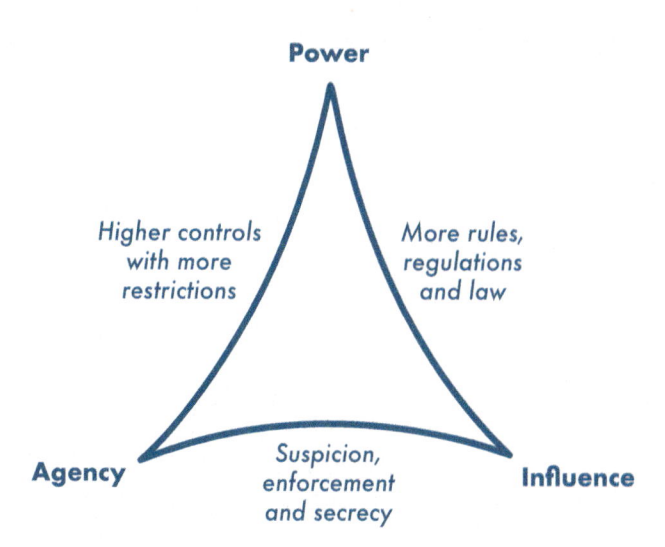

Figure 2: Destructive Relationships

```
                        Power
                          ▲
                         ╱ ╲
         Higher controls ╱   ╲ More rules,
           with more    ╱     ╲ regulations
          restrictions ╱       ╲ and law
                      ╱         ╲
                     ╱           ╲
   Agency ──────────────────────── Influence
                 Suspicion,
                 enforcement
                 and secrecy
```

What this scenario begins to show is that when each of the players in a destructive loop behaves destructively, it becomes a near-impossible cycle to escape. What may be less evident, is that if one player acts destructively, and in their own interests, all the other players will start to act in their own interests, and the destructive cycle will evolve. The player who starts a destructive cycle could be the influencer, seeking a more significant role; the person in power wanting more control over their agents; or the person with agency, who wishes to hide, and not be transparent. When we look instead at the constructive cycle, we can see that if all the players act constructively, there's a very different outcome - but, this requires all of the players to continue to act constructively, to keep the cycle going. A diversion into game theory would be prudent here if this chapter were an entire book.

Starting with the same prime mover, the "influencer", let's now consider a constructive cycle. This is summarised in Figure 3, *Constructive Relationships*.

In this scenario, the influencer believes in a smaller, lighter-touch regulator doing the right thing - they believe more strongly in education and rights. The influencer might approach the person with power, and, rather than demanding more rules and regulations, they suggest that the person with power should educate and give more freedom to the person with agency.

In this case, those with agency can respond by effectively giving the person with power even more power, through the freedom that's been granted to them. By example, highly competitive markets in capitalist-based economies (transport, entertainment, leisure, utilities) have become less regulated. Still, aspects of the delivery and operations, such as health and safety, remain highly regulated.

Further, in a constructive cycle, the person with agency will likely have an open and trusting relationship with the person with influence. It could be likely, as the agency/ influencer relationship is one of relative transparency. The influencer, because they can determine what the person with agency is doing by, say, API access to the dataset, can instruct the person with power on the right types of education that the market needs. Further, they can consider the rights[33] to be offered to the various people with agency in the market, who can use their freedom to construct a better society, which in turn builds more trusting relationships.

> What leads to relationships becoming constructive - as in, better decisions and better outcomes?

Figure 3: Constructive Relationships

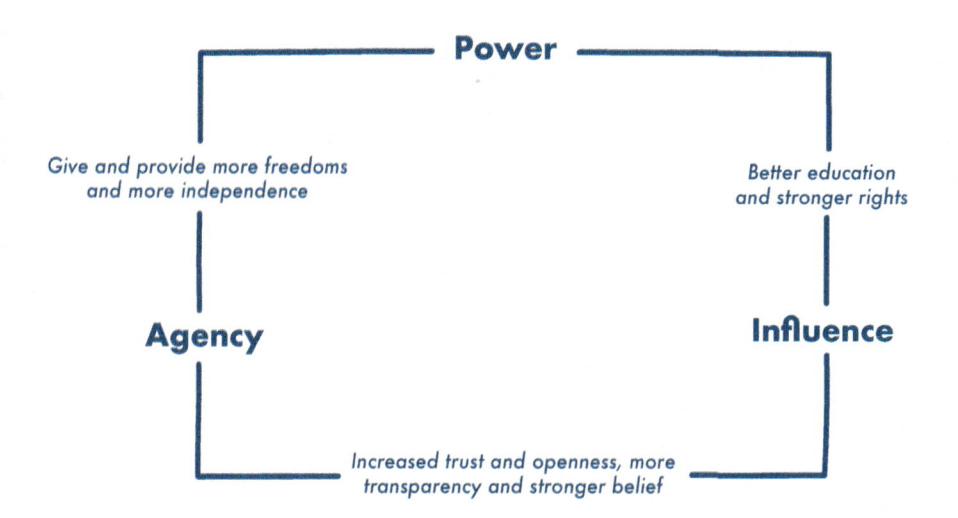

```
                         Power
        ┌─────────────────┴─────────────────┐
        │                                   │
Give and provide more freedoms      Better education
   and more independence           and stronger rights
        │                                   │
     Agency                             Influence
        │                                   │
        │    Increased trust and openness, more    │
        └──── transparency and stronger belief ────┘
```

Contrasting the two cycles, constructive and destructive, the obvious question is what leads to a constructive or a destructive outcome? Further, in each cycle, do the consequences get better or worse for all players? In the destructive cycle, it could be argued that the outcome for the influencer is hugely beneficial, as they end up with a larger regulatory body, more market kudos and an increase in their income.

Equally, the person with power may believe that this route enables them to raise more tax income. So, if we look purely at outcomes, it depends on which outcomes for whom we are looking at, as to how we make the judgement of who benefits from a constructive or destructive cycle. Consider - do we want better outcomes for humanity and society, or just a few players?

This new framework for power, agency and influence aims to set oversight and governance in a different context. The current governance thinking for a regulated industry is biased towards more rules and increasing regulation and law. Given the political design, is this driven by a desire to change the behaviour of those with agency? If so, we may not end up with the outcomes we intended to create – better banking, transport or utilities. In contrast, the current governmental thinking on unregulated industries is more liberal.

Still, that thinking has not generated better outcomes for society – as we have seen with climate change and the broken supply chain model resulting from the pandemic. The reason for presenting this new framework is to reflect on the question "is this working for us?". As shown in earlier chapters, it is clear that the current cycles of governance and oversight are not working, for regulated or unregulated industries. Therefore, we need to think about a future of governance that can take us forward from where we are – and does not just do more of the same.

Figures 3 and 4 Combined:

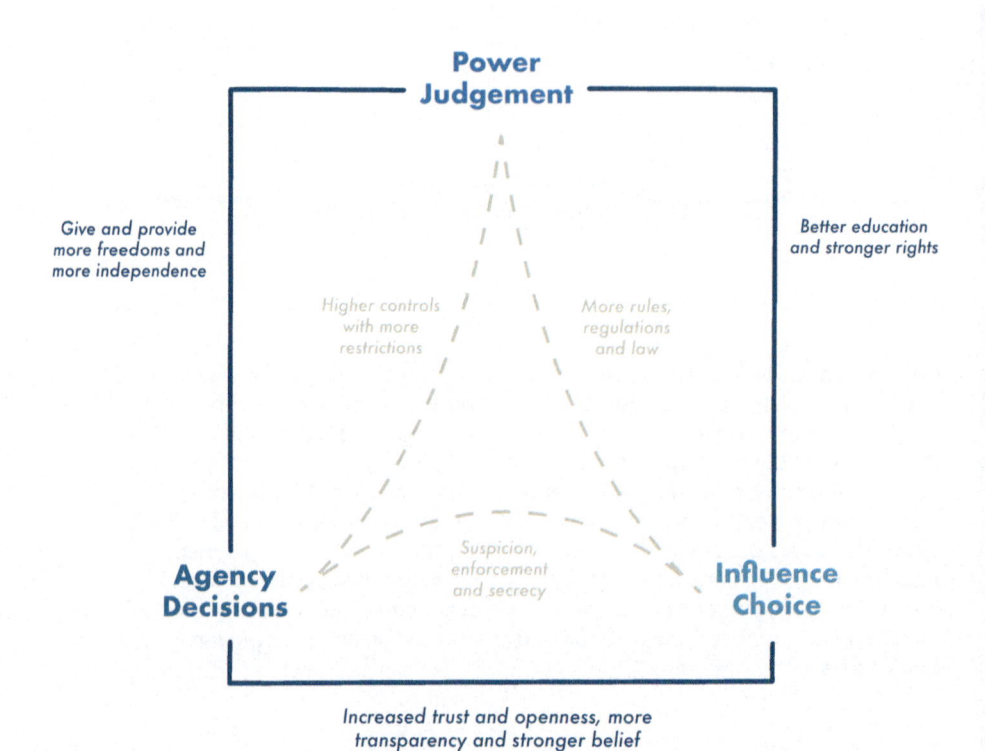

Power
Judgement

Give and provide more freedoms and more independence

Higher controls with more restrictions

More rules, regulations and law

Better education and stronger rights

Suspicion, enforcement and secrecy

Agency
Decisions

Influence
Choice

Increased trust and openness, more transparency and stronger belief

In Figure 4, *Board Relationships*, this model is used to consider the set of relationships between shareholders, directors, and the executive team.

Whilst figure 4 shows that power rests with the shareholders, equally, power can be held by the directors or exec team; agency can rest with the shareholders and executive team; and influence, with the shareholders or directors. Every combination is possible. The point here is less about the possible scenarios and relationships, but rather to pay extra attention to the special case where a founder is a director, major shareholder and CEO.

Figure 4: Board Relationships

Power
Shareholders

Agency
Directors

Influence
Executive Team

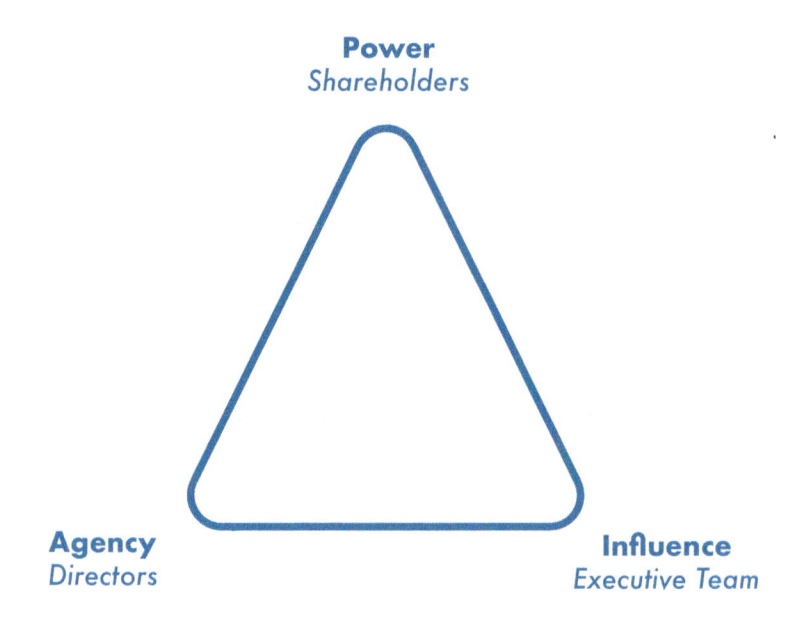

In the special cases where a team is able to hold all three - power, agency and influence - there is a significant increase in the need for better governance, and increased oversight given to outside parties, so that decisions are fair, reasonable, explainable and have wider benefits beyond that of the team's immediate gain.

It is worth drawing on a personal experience with a commercial, charity or health situation, and using this power, agency and influence framework to think about how the actors act to create better outcomes, and for who - say, the capital providers.

Chapter 5

Revising the S-Curve in an age of emergence

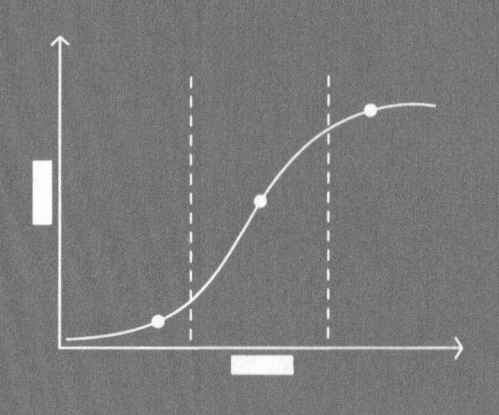

Exploring how the S-Curve can help us with leadership, strategy and decision making in an age of emergence (an age observed when an entity or system displays properties or behaviours which interact as part of an inclusive whole).

History and context

There is a special place in our business hearts and minds for the "S" curve or Sigmoid function[34], calling it by its proper maths name. The origin of the S curve[35] goes back to the study of population growth by Pierre-François Verhulst[36] published c.1838. Verhulst was influenced by Thomas Malthus' "An Essay on the Principle of Population" which showed that growth of a biological population is self-limiting by the finite amount of available resources. The logistic equation is also sometimes called the Verhulst-Pearl equation, following its rediscovery in 1920. Alfred J. Lotka derived the equation again in 1925, calling it the law of population growth, but he is now better known for his predator:prey model[37].

Figure 1: Bohlen and Beal's Diffusion process

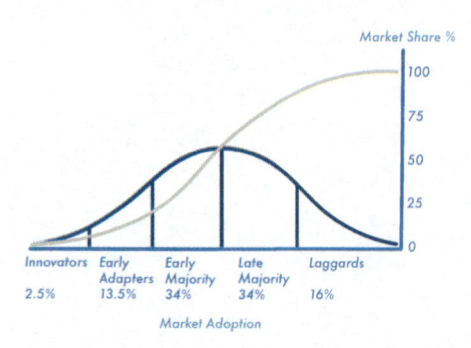

Innovators	Early Adapters	Early Majority	Late Majority	Laggards
2.5%	13.5%	34%	34%	16%

Market Adoption

In 1957, business strategists Joe Bohlen and George Beal published the Diffusion Process[38] – taking the adoption curve[39] and adding the cumulative take up of the product to gain a "classic S-Curve."

Figure 2: Classic market adoption curve

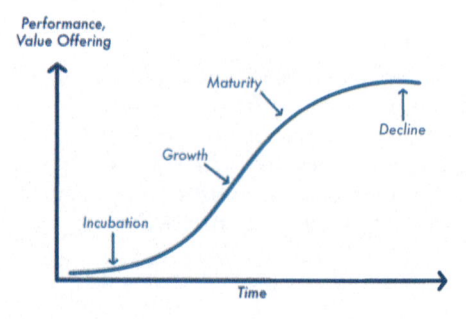

This market adoption curve became the basis for explaining innovation and growth as a broader market-based economic concept by the late 1960s. We started to consider the importance of incubation of ideas to create new businesses, and how we need a flow of products/ services within big companies.

From this thinking emerged two concepts, and meanwhile, the shareholder primacy model became central to growth. The first concept is "Curve Jumping" - ensuring that you continue to grow by keeping shareholders happy through the continuous introduction of new products, as the existing ones have matured. Of course, the downside is that if a business cannot jump, because of its current cost base or ability to adopt the latest technology to perpetuate the ascension of the curve, new companies will instead emerge with competitive advantages (product or cost) as they jump to new technologies.

Milton Friedman's[40] emphasis on shareholder value maximisation at the expense of other considerations has driven companies to keep up with the next curve, by fear of being left behind competitively. Some types of competition are healthier for markets than others. It appears that in this case, competition and anxiety relating to retaining technology leadership at all costs have been driving capitalism in a particularly destructive direction, rather than encouraging useful, sustainable and friendly innovation. There is an economics essay to be written here, but this chapter focuses specifically on the S-Curve.

Figure 3: Curve jumping in business

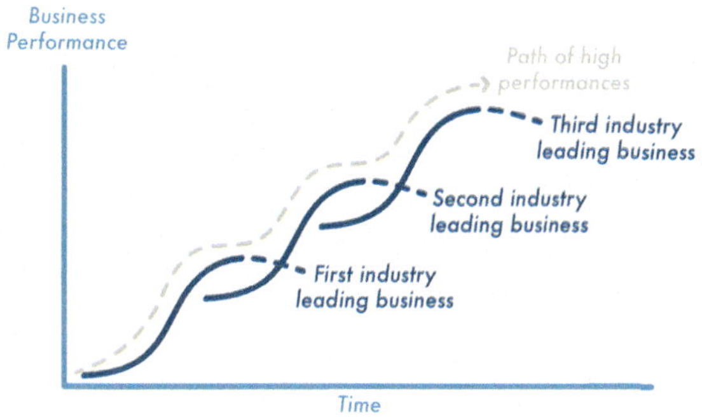

Right here, right now

We live in a time when many crises and systematic "emergent properties" are gaining attention and prominence. Emergence, by definition, occurs when an entity or system is observed to have properties that its parts do not pose or display on their own.

When properties or behaviours only emerge when the parts interact in the broader system, as we see in our businesses, we understand these to be complex adaptive systems.

Shareholder primacy as an economic driver faded in 1990, to be replaced finally in 2019 with Colin Mayer's[41] work on the Purpose Model[42], a modern standard for corporate responsibility which makes an equal commitment to all stakeholders. However, shareholder primacy's simplicity has remained a stalwart of leadership training and teaching, and therefore, management thinking. Its simplicity meant we did not have to deal with the contradictions and conflicting requirements that a broader business purpose would expose. The Business Roundtable August 2019 statement[43] and Blackrock CEO Larry Fink's letters to CEOs/Shareholders are critical milestones in turning mainstream thinking away from considering pure shareholder returns as the reason for a business to exist.

The current shift is towards ecosystem sustainability and ESG (Environmental sustainability, Social responsibility and better oversight and Governance) as primary drivers. The FCA Stewardship[44] code, Section 172 of the companies act[45] and decision reporting are some of the first legislative instruments on this journey. With now over 50 series A funded startups active in ESG reporting, impact investing has become a meme as the development of a more standardised and comprehensive purpose reporting has strengthened.

> **Shareholder primacy's simplicity meant we did not have to deal with the contradictions and conflicting requirements that a broader business purpose would expose.**

With this new framing, it is time to revisit the S-Curve.

Framing the S-Curve for an evolutionary journey

If you have not yet discovered Simon Wardley[46] and his mapping thinking[47], stop here and watch this video[48]. Simon has demonstrated a brilliant S-Curve model, including pioneers, settlers and town planners; it is really worth looking up. His model[49] focuses on evolution (journey towards a commodity) rather than diffusion (take up over time). To quote Simon *"The evolution of a single act from genesis to commodity may involve hundreds if not thousands of diffusion curves for each evolving instance of that act, each with their own chasm."*

In the S-Curve below, an evolution S-Curve, I am building on Simon's axis of ubiquity[50] (how common something is) and certainty[51] (the likelihood of the outcome being as determined). On the below axes, we are plotting the development of companies and their systems - time is not present, but as we will see, we have to remove time from the framing.

Starting at the bottom left, we have the activity of innovation - where ubiquity is low, as innovation is still an idea, so it is not available to everyone. The certainty that any innovation will work is also low.

Figure 4: Adaptation and adoption of processes on the route to scale

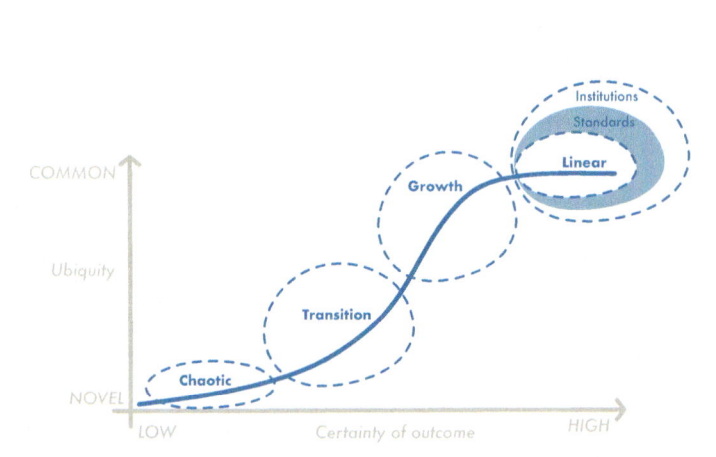

Chaotic
Activity: INNOVATION
Practice: NOVEL/NEW
Data: COLLECTED
Control: LEAN, MVP
Model: MESSY

Transition
Activity: BESPOKE
Practice: EMERGENT
Data: STRUCTURED
Control: AGILE & SCRUM
Model: LIMITED

Growth
Activity: PRODUCT
Practice: GOOD
Data: LINKED/RELATIONAL
Control: PRINCE 2
Model: PREDICTIVE & STABLE

Linear
Activity: COMMODITY AT SCALE
Practice: BEST
Data: MODELLED & AI
Control: 6 SIGMA & KPI
Model: DECISION MAKING

The top right corner is the perceived Northstar. In a Northstar context, ubiquity is high, as everyone is involved, and there is high certainty that the business will succeed. This top right corner includes commodities, utilities, and technologies deployed at scale - for example, that enable us to turn on the tap and drink water as it flows. Linking innovation ("Chaotic") and commodity ("Linear") is an evolution or journey S-Curve. This curve depicts the transformation of the company, including the company's practices, data, controls, and the models it will most likely utilise. In addition, the chart below highlights the most popular thinking of businesses at each stage, but is certainly not exclusive. Agile works well in all phases, AI can be used anywhere except in choice[52], and data is not as definite as the bubbles in the above graph would suggest. Methods of control change as we evolve from lean/ MVP in the first delivery, to using methodologies such as agile and scrum, Prince 2 as a grown-up project management tool at scale, and then towards quality management with 6 Sigma.

Note: I have a passionate dislike of the term "best practice" as it only applies when in the linear (last) phase, but is often mentioned at every stage. At linear, you have the evidence and data to support what "best" looks like. At any stage before ubiquity and certainty, best practice is simply not possible, other than by lucking out. A desire for best practice ignores all that you have to learn and prove before you find what is "best". And to all those who are there - you can still do better, so how can it truly be "best"?

Figure 5: Business systems at each stage of growth

	ACTIVITY	PRACTICE	DATA	CONTROL	BUSINESS MODEL
CHAOTIC	Innovation	Novel and new	Collection is a priority	Lean/MVP	Messy
TRANSITION	Bespoke Product/Service	Emergent	Structured	Agile and scrum	Limited
GROWTH	Product that complies	Good	Linked/ Relational	PRINCE 2	Predictive and stable
LINEAR	Commodity at scale	Best	Modelled with AI	6 Sigma & API	Decision making

When one considers the idea of time and S-Curves, you get to curve jumping or continual product development, as set out earlier. The evolution or journey S-Curve, when presented in this way, demonstrates that when time is not the axis, any significant business will have all these activities present at all times (continual adaptation/ evolution, not diffusion). In nature, all levels of species exist at the same time - from single cell to complex organisms. Innovation is not a destination; it is a journey, in which you have to operate at all camps along the route, at the same time.

> **Innovation is not a destination; it is a journey, in which you have to operate at all camps along the route, at the same time.**

Evolution S-Curve and governance

Harvard Business Review (HBR) argues that most capitalist markets are in a post-shareholder primacy model[53], meaning the primary purpose of an organisation is now up for debate. It appears that companies are en route to a more inclusive purpose and reason to exist[54].

Law regarding directors' duties already exists in the UK in the form of Section 172 of the Companies Act[55]. The global pandemic has highlighted significant weaknesses that emerge from our focus on growth and shareholder returns, including the following examples:

1. Highly integrated long supply chains are incredibly efficient, but are very brittle and lack resilience - when broken, we lose effectiveness.

2. A business needs to re-balance towards effectiveness. A food company in a pandemic exists to get food to customers (effectiveness) - not to drive efficiency at any cost.

3. Ecosystem sustainability is more important than any single company's fortunes.

4. Managing ESG, risk, being better ancestors, and tackling climate change - these are all extremely difficult for one single company to take on.

5. Our existing risk models focus on resource allocation, safety and control, and not the topics mentioned above. This framing means that new risk created in a digital-first world may be outside of the frame, and therefore, hidden in plain sight.

Given this framing and context, it is worth overlaying governance on the S-curve of start-up development, which we will now unpack.

Figure 6: Adding Governance

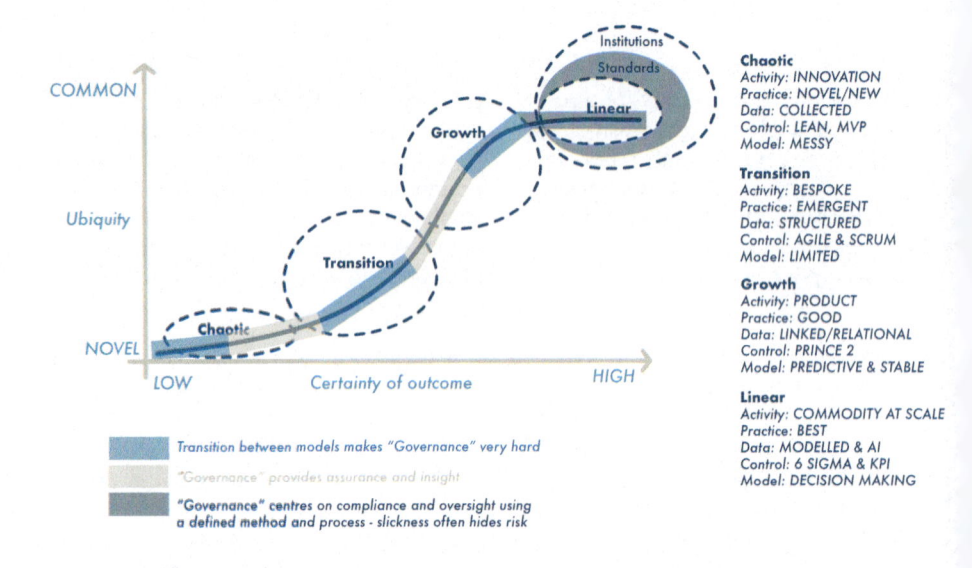

Chart axes: Y-axis "Ubiquity" from NOVEL to COMMON; X-axis "Certainty of outcome" from LOW to HIGH. Curve passes through stages: Chaotic → Transition → Growth → Linear (with Standards and Institutions).

Legend:
- Transition between models makes "Governance" very hard
- "Governance" provides assurance and insight
- "Governance" centres on compliance and oversight using a defined method and process - slickness often hides risk

Chaotic
Activity: INNOVATION
Practice: NOVEL/NEW
Data: COLLECTED
Control: LEAN, MVP
Model: MESSY

Transition
Activity: BESPOKE
Practice: EMERGENT
Data: STRUCTURED
Control: AGILE & SCRUM
Model: LIMITED

Growth
Activity: PRODUCT
Practice: GOOD
Data: LINKED/RELATIONAL
Control: PRINCE 2
Model: PREDICTIVE & STABLE

Linear
Activity: COMMODITY AT SCALE
Practice: BEST
Data: MODELLED & AI
Control: 6 SIGMA & KPI
Model: DECISION MAKING

Governance has historically focussed on corporates and large companies, offering products and services to mass markets. Governance, with independence of oversight, has been concentrated on companies that are operating at scale and are well managed. We have ultimately framed governance as only necessary where there is an interest to wider society regarding corporate behaviour. Indeed, it becomes a burden rather than being of value.

Companies operating at scale tend to be found in the linear quadrant (top right) of the above graph, where growth is mainly incremental and linear. Regulation and markets focus on reaching "BEST" practices, which have been derived over a long period. The data used is highly modelled, and the application of AI creates new opportunities and value. Control is exercised through the utilisation of 6 Sigma for quality (repeatability) and other advanced program management techniques. KPIs enable the delegation of actions, and the monitoring and control thereof. The business model is that of exercising good or "best" decision making, based on ideas of resource allocation and risk.

Corporate governance[56] is a broad and thorny topic, but understanding foundations such as The Cadbury Report (1992)[57] and the Sarbanes–Oxley Act[58] (2002) is crucial, as they have been instrumental in framing mandates. Confusingly, governance, compliance and risk management[59] became one topic in c.2007 and lost the clear separation of function. In addition to those mentioned, regulation has also formed an effective backstop to control behaviours and market abuse.

The point is, when a company is operating at scale, we have created *"best governance practices and guidance"*, along with excellent risk frameworks and stewardship codes for investors. Many of the tools and methods have stood the test of time and provided confidence to the market. However, these tools and frameworks are only designed for those companies operating at scale. On the journey from start-up to scale, the adoption of such heavyweight practices in early development would be overly burdensome for emergent companies, and are not a best or a good fit.

We must remember that any company of significant scale can operate within all the phases displayed in the above graph. However, there are five possible camps or phases where we need governance; three are represented in the previous graph in light blue, and two in beige. The beige blocks represent phases where there is a degree of stability (there can be growth, but no absolute changes). Contrastingly, the light blue block represents phases where everything is changing. Beige blocks indicate somewhat predictable, but complicated oversight, where light blue suggests a complex emerging state.

To be clear, it is not that companies or markets in a linear phase are not complex; it is that management in a linear phase has more certainty in terms of practices and forecasting, and often deals with less change. When there is a product of service at "linear", it delivers significant, noisy signals and creates priorities that often overshadow those created from any data or insights from other phases. Management, at scale, requires an understanding of the delta between the plan and the executed outcome, and the ability to make minor adjustments to continually optimise performance.

The management during the beige stable growth camps/ phases is complicated, as patterns and data will not always be that useful. Data will not be able to point to a definitive decision directly. Governance provides assurance and insights as management continually searches for the correct data to make decisions on, which may not even exist. Within the light blue highly volatile camps/ phases, management is more complicated, as we cannot rely on existing data during the transition to new frontiers. Simply put, if we rely on existing data, we will be unable to move on to the new. The idea of transition is that the old is left behind. Experienced leadership will seek small signals from both the noisy existing data and the new data. When considering governance through these dynamic phases, it is apparent that it becomes much more challenging, and that we cannot rely on the wisdom and best practices of linear.

Governance plans at scale are more comfortable and more predictable; they are designed to enable the measurement of a delta. Plans during innovation phases are precisely the opposite - not easy and highly unpredictable. Using the same word "plan" in both cases means we lose definition and distinction.

- A plan at scale is built on years of data and modelled to be highly reliable; it is accurate and has a level of detail that can create KPIs for reporting. The plan and the model is a fantastic prediction tool.

- A plan at start-up and growth is about direction and intention. Failure to have one would be catastrophic, but within the first few hours of the words being committed to a shared document, the plan is out of date. To be useful, it must lack precision, detail and measurement, but will instead set out stages, actions and outcomes. It must have a purpose and direction, to frame complex decisions.

Similarly, governance at scale is more comfortable and more predictable; governance is about understanding where and how a delta might arise, and being ready for it. Governance during innovation is precisely the opposite - not easy and highly unpredictable.

> **Using the same word "Governance" at scale and in start-up cases means we lose definition and distinction.**

Complexity: organisational mash-ups

Many businesses are mash-ups of previous transformations[60] plus current evolution. This observation has two ramifications: one, the structure, processes and skills of a business are neither fully aligned to the original model, or various constructions of a new model. Two, data shows that as you review focus and alignment of those in the more senior positions, and who have been in post the longest, most have a compass or alignment coupled with a mash-up of a previous model. Bluntly, they stopped on the evolutionary path, creating a dead end. Senior management with a closed mindset, rather than an open and continually learning one, tend to fall back on the experience of previous best practices, models and pre-transformational ideals, adding a significant burden to governance for any stage. The idea that there is a direct coupling between innovation and KPI measurement, which makes it harder for corporations to innovate and evolve, is explored in chapter 3, "Are KPIs the nemesis of innovation?".

All companies have an increasing dependence on wider business ecosystems for their growth and survival. Organisational ecosystem health[61] is critical for companies at scale with extensive supply chains and customer bases. Companies who operate at scale and in the linear phase, therefore, are dependent on companies who are in different stages on a planned route to scale. Thus, not only is a large-scale company dealing with its internal governance and innovation requirements, as already noted, but the Directors have to understand data from the wider business ecosystem, who are also trying to understand what their data is telling them about their evolutionary path.

Directors have to understand data from the wider business ecosystem, who are also trying to understand what their data is telling them about their evolutionary path.

Governance is not about best practices and processes at any stage; it is about the mindset of an entire organisation, and now, the wider ecosystem. When you reflect on it, directors with governance responsibilities must cope with and process data for decision making from chaotic and linear requirements at the same time — relying on individuals and teams who have different perceptions, both inside and outside of the organisation. Never has data-sharing[62] been more important as a concept, and it can be used as a tool for collaboration, or a weapon (inaccurate data) in competitive markets. How can a director know that the data they get from their surrounding business ecosystem can support their decision making and enable complex judgements?

Take away

The S-curve has helped us on several journeys thus far. It supported our understanding of adoption and growth; it can now be critical in helping us understand the development and evolution of governance towards a sustainable future[63]. An evolutionary S-curve is more applicable than ever as we enter a new phase of emergence. Our resulting actions and behaviours emerge when we grasp that all parts of our local business ecosystem interact as a comprehensive whole.

A governance S-curve can help us unpack new risks in this dependent ecosystem, so that we can make better judgements that lead to better outcomes. What is evident is that we need far more than proof, lineage and provenance of data from the wider ecosystem if we are going to create better decision-making environments - we need a new data management platform. Such a new platform is my current focus, and why I am working on Digital20[64].

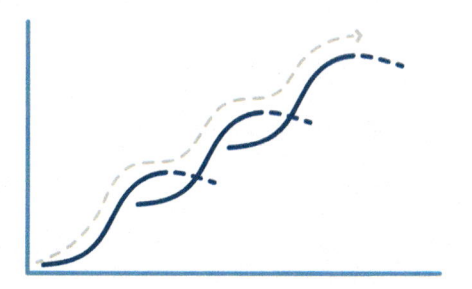

Chapter 6

Humans want principles, society demands rules and businesses want to manage risk.

Can we reconcile the differences?

The linkage between principles and rules is often not clear - this is because we have created so many words and variances in our language that there is significant confusion between the terms. As humans, we are inconsistent in how we apply words and language, often to provide a benefit to ourselves, or justify a held belief. To unpack the relationship between principles and rules, we need to first understand definitions - but we must accept that even definitions are inconsistent. Our confirmation bias will fight against our increased understanding, as we want to believe what we already know, rather than expanding our thinking.

Are we imagining principles or values?

It is worth noting that our principles are defined by our values. This is much like ethics (group beliefs) and morals (personal beliefs), and how, in a complex adaptive system, my morals affect the group's ethics and the group's ethics in turn change my morals.

Situational awareness and experience play a significant part in what you believe right now, and what your wider group or society believes.

Figure 1: Values and principles

VALUES	PRINCIPLES
- Values are qualities or standards of behaviour - Values help us to form principles - Values are not stern, ridgid or fixed; they can adapt	- Principles are beliefs that govern our behaviour - Principles are based on our values - Principles tend to be identified as rules, which provide control - Principles are stern and unyielding

Values can be adaptable to a specific context, whereas principles are fixed for a period, withstanding the test of time. Setting up a framework to determine our principles implies that we don't want them to change every day, week, month, year - that they are good and stable for a generation - but that we can adapt/ revise/ adjust our principles, based on new learning.

Fundamentally, principles are based on values, which do change, so there are ebbs and flows of conflict between the two. This means that we frame principles and often refuse to see that they are not eternally future proof. Indeed, the further a principle is away from the time it was created, the less it will have in common with our values.

△ ○ ◇ □

Are we confusing principles and rules?

Characteristically, principles are abstract and universal, whereas a rule is specific and particular. Principles can cope with exceptions; rules need another rule. Principles enable the power of thought and decision making; rules prevent individual thought and discretion.

Principles need knowledge and experience to deliver outcomes; rules don't. Principles cope with risk, conflict and abstraction; whereas conflict is not possible for a rule - it is this rule or another rule is needed.

Figure 2: Rules and principles

RULES	PRINCIPLES
- One size fits all	- Decisions are made based on the alignment of each case to the principle
- Easy, anyone can do it (instruction)	- Difficult to craft; requires time, skill and thought
- Efficient but not effective	- Effective, although at times not efficient
- A large number of rules are needed	- A few principles cover the majority of situations
- Applying the same thinking in every case has the appearance of consistency, but points to inconsistency in organisational values	- Making case-by-case decisions has the appearance of inconsistency, but over time results in decisions that are consistent with organisational values
- Focused on compliance, easy to enforce	- Focused on behaviour that demonstrates commitment
- Preferred by all when trust is low	- Preferred by all when trust is high
- Rigid, built to avoid change	- Flexible in changing contexts, a guideline
- Constraining, and provide control	- Empowering
- Focussed on the processes and activities	- Focused on results and positive culture, embraces change
- Rules create gofers	- Principles cultivate stewardship and ownership

The word itself, "rule", needs some more unpacking, as it can take on many meanings. The etymology of the word "rule" is summarised here[65].

The choice of "rule" is designed to be ambitious, allowing you, the reader, to apply your own context, thereby creating more relevance to your own circumstances.

Figure 3: Unpacking the ontology of the word 'rule'

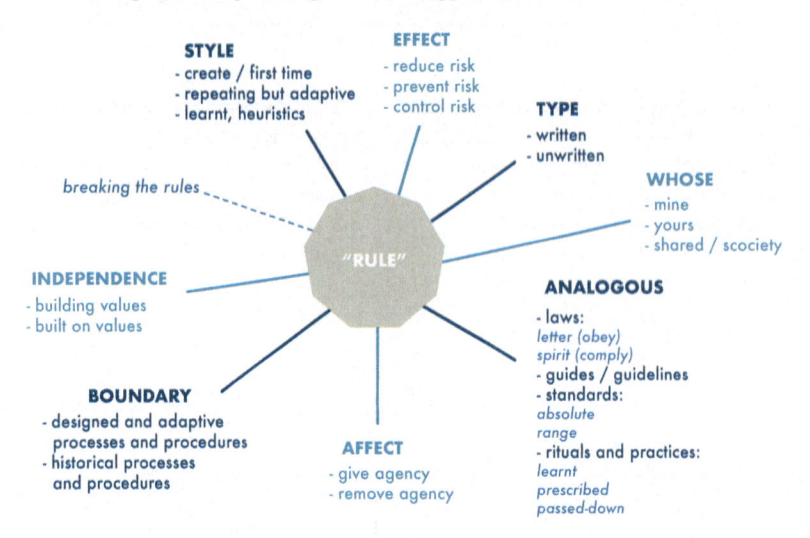

STYLE
- create / first time
- repeating but adaptive
- learnt, heuristics

EFFECT
- reduce risk
- prevent risk
- control risk

TYPE
- written
- unwritten

WHOSE
- mine
- yours
- shared / scociety

breaking the rules

"RULE"

ANALOGOUS
- laws:
  letter (obey)
  spirit (comply)
- guides / guidelines
- standards:
  absolute
  range
- rituals and practices:
  learnt
  prescribed
  passed-down

INDEPENDENCE
- building values
- built on values

BOUNDARY
- designed and adaptive processes and procedures
- historical processes and procedures

AFFECT
- give agency
- remove agency

What is evident is that the concept of "rule" is contextual to an individual, which means that for me, you or someone else, a rule can mean any of the following, and indeed many of them at the same time;

- Rules are written, unwritten, or both

- Rules are mine, created by me, that you need to follow. They are yours, crafted by you, that you need me to obey. They are shared, and we believe that they create a better society

- Rules can be the law; just a guide; the standard you need to meet; or the rituals that create success. But which law, the one that we should not break or the one by which we follow the spirit? As a guide, but to guide me from here to where? As a standard - is that absolute, or is a range good enough? My rituals - did I learn them, did you teach me, or somehow are they just there?

- Rules equally give you more freedom (safety, lower risk of murder) and remove your freedom (choice). Rules give me more agency, and at the same time, remove it.

- Rules define my boundaries. But have I created rules for myself and continually refined them as I learn, or are my rules ones that come from history (because we have always done it this way)?

- Do my rules define my values, or are my rules the manifestation of someone else's values?

- Rules are only there to be broken

- Rules allow me to create something as I have done something, gained experience, and learned. Rules help me to not make the same mistake, and improve and adapt. Rules save me time and energy - I love my heuristics

- Rules allow me to manage, prevent and control risk.

But whose rules are they?

Back to the relationship between rules and principles. In companies and social policy, we can set rules and principles into a matrix, as below. To help us to define where social norms stop, and laws are needed, we should ask where it is better to break rules or comply - and to uphold principles, or to challenge them.

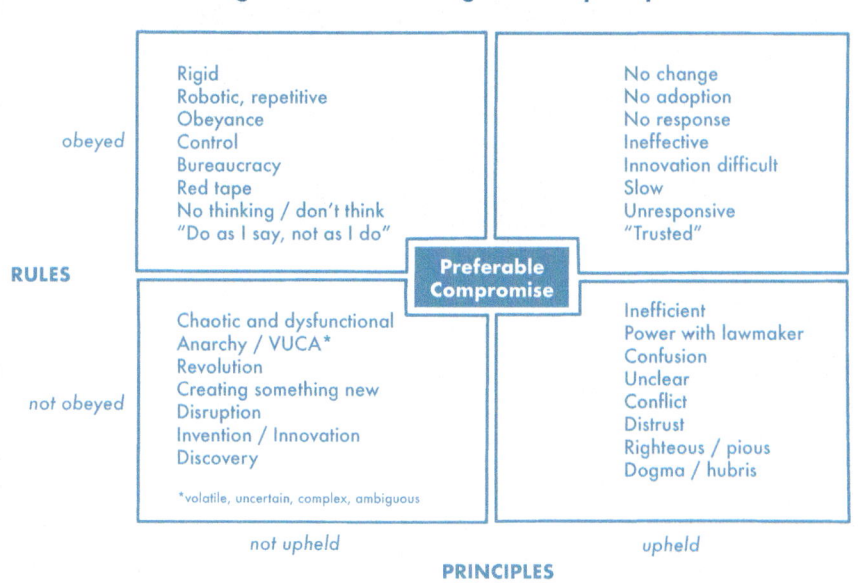

Figure 4: Understanding rules and principles

	not upheld	upheld
obeyed	Rigid Robotic, repetitive Obeyance Control Bureaucracy Red tape No thinking / don't think "Do as I say, not as I do"	No change No adoption No response Ineffective Innovation difficult Slow Unresponsive "Trusted"
not obeyed	Chaotic and dysfunctional Anarchy / VUCA* Revolution Creating something new Disruption Invention / Innovation Discovery	Inefficient Power with lawmaker Confusion Unclear Conflict Distrust Righteous / pious Dogma / hubris

Preferable Compromise (between top-right and bottom-left quadrants)

*volatile, uncertain, complex, ambiguous

RULES (vertical axis) / **PRINCIPLES** (horizontal axis)

A review of the above four quadrants highlights that there is no favourable sector, and indeed, as a society seeking improvement, we continually travel through all of them. A contradiction is realised when companies and executives feel that upholding principles and obeying rules (top right) creates the best culture, but also ask their organisations to be adaptive, agile and innovative.

Given that principles are based on values, the leadership team will be instrumental in ensuring that principles are upheld. Whilst the company's level of documentation for processes, procedures and rules will define what is to be obeyed, the culture of the top team will determine if they are to be obeyed, or not.

The below matrix looks at combinations of values and principles. Here, values are either mine as an individual or "ours" as a collective society.

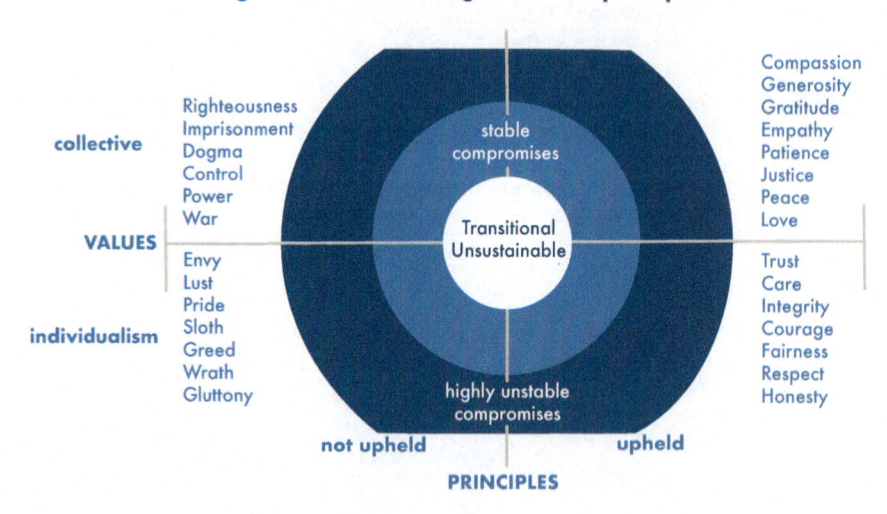

Figure 5: Understanding values and principles

	not upheld	upheld
collective (VALUES)	Righteousness, Imprisonment, Dogma, Control, Power, War	Compassion, Generosity, Gratitude, Empathy, Patience, Justice, Peace, Love
individualism (VALUES)	Envy, Lust, Pride, Sloth, Greed, Wrath, Gluttony	Trust, Care, Integrity, Courage, Fairness, Respect, Honesty

Rings (inner to outer): Transitional Unsustainable; stable compromises / highly unstable compromises.

PRINCIPLES

The fundamental issue with these two representations (rules/ values, and principles) is that they cannot highlight the dynamic nature of the relationship between each one. For example, our collective values help normalise individual bias, and those collective values inform and refine our collective principles. Indeed, as principles become extreme and too restrictive (perhaps because our collective values become too godly), our collective values opt to no longer uphold those principles. When our individualism leads to the falling apart of society, we raise the collective standard of our virtues as it makes us feel more content, loved, and at peace.

The "stable compromise" domain summarises this movement, and has been explored many times, and the Tytler cycle of history[66] was probably one of the first. The Tytler cycle is a theory that all governments, regardless of their form, will eventually collapse and be replaced by a new government. The cycle is said to consist of eight stages: bondage, spiritual faith, great courage, liberty, abundance, selfishness, complacency, apathy, and dependence. The cycle is said to repeat itself every 200 years or so.

Tytler argued that the cycle is inevitable because human nature is flawed. He believed that people are naturally selfish and lazy, and that they will eventually take advantage of their freedoms and become corrupt. This corruption will lead to the collapse of the government, and the cycle will start again. The Tytler cycle is a controversial theory, and there is no scientific evidence to support it. However, it is a reminder that all governments are fragile, and that they must be constantly vigilant to prevent their collapse.

Figure 6: Tytler cycle of history

- **Bondage** - people oppose their conditions
- **Faith** - search for unity / deep moral gatherings
- **Courage** - people fight for freedom
- **Liberty** - prosperity and freedom achieved
- **Abundance** - focus turns to material things
- **Selfishness** - "It's all about me and my stuff"
- **Complacency** - entitlement and self-absorption
- **Apathy** - PERSONAL RESPONSIBILITY LOST "It's not my fault"
- **Dependence** - freedom centralised / independence controlled
- **POINT OF NO RETURN** Government achieves complete control

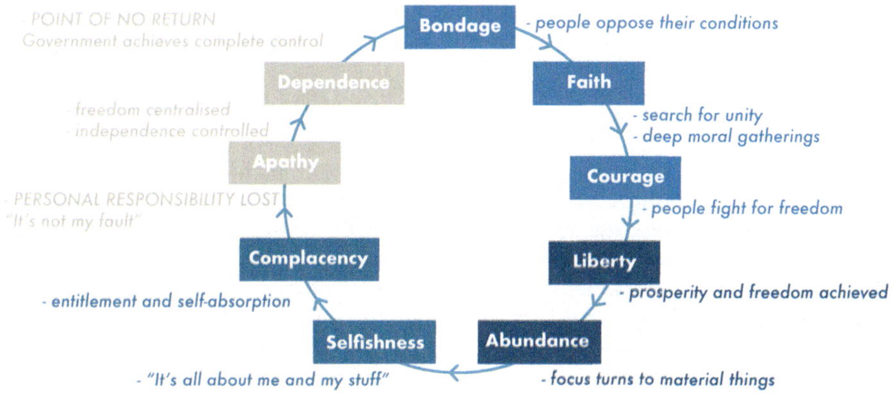

In summary, a rules-based approach prescribes or describes in detail a set of rules and behaviour stipulations, based on known and agreed principles. In contrast, a principle-based approach sets the boundaries that enable controls, measures, and procedures that achieve an outcome to be left for each organisation to determine.

Risk frameworks help us to connect principles and rules

So far, we have explored that a rules-based approach prescribes in detail the rules, methods, procedures, processes and tasks for how to behave and act; whereas a principle-based approach to creating outcomes frames boundaries, leaving the individual or organisation to determine its own way forward.

- In a theoretical linear system, we would agree on principles, which would bound the rules.

- In a nonlinear system, we would agree on the principles, which would bound the rules; and as we learn from the rules, we would refine the principles.

- In the reality of a complex adaptive system, responses to rules evolve, so the rules must be continually modified, causing our values and subsequently our principles to change, and repeating the cycle.

This chapter is titled "**Humans want principles, society demands rules and businesses want to manage risk**". The obvious relationship between the three is that rules change values, which change principles, which means our rules need to be updated. However, this process of learning and adoption depends on understanding the connection between the three, which enables closed-loop feedback. **Our risk frameworks enable this understanding.**

The diagram below places rules and principles at two extremes. As already explored, we move from principles to rules but rarely go back to rethink our principles, mostly because of the constraints of time. Rules should refine and improve in real-time, whereas principles are generational.

When reviewing our rules, we use and apply a risk framework. The risk framework identifies risk and helps us manage it, and in turn, we use rules to ensure that we get the right data/information to be able to determine if we have control over risk. As humans, we are not experts in forecasting the unimagined, and so, when we implement rules, some will not work and clever minds will bend, break or avoid many of them. To that end, we create more rules to manage those exceptions. However, occasionally we need to check that our rules are still aligned to our principles - and revisit and refine those principles.

Figure 7: Rules and principles at two extremes

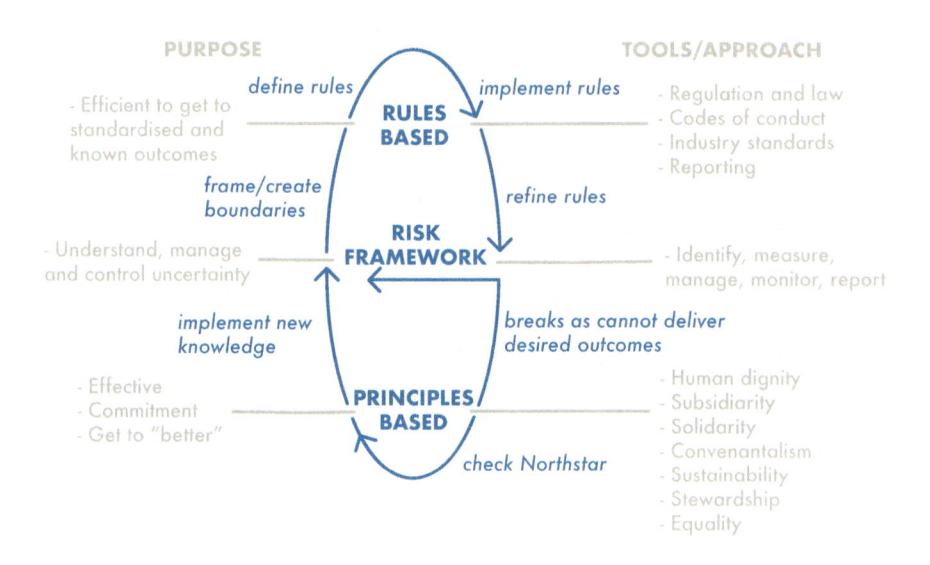

PURPOSE

- Efficient to get to standardised and known outcomes

- Understand, manage and control uncertainty

- Effective
- Commitment
- Get to "better"

RULES BASED — define rules / implement rules

RISK FRAMEWORK — frame/create boundaries / refine rules

PRINCIPLES BASED — implement new knowledge / breaks as cannot deliver desired outcomes / check Northstar

TOOLS/APPROACH

- Regulation and law
- Codes of conduct
- Industry standards
- Reporting

- Identify, measure, manage, monitor, report

- Human dignity
- Subsidiarity
- Solidarity
- Convenantalism
- Sustainability
- Stewardship
- Equality

Starting from a principles-based approach, this is anchored in ideas such as human dignity[67], subsidiarity[68], solidarity[69], convenantalism[70], sustainability[71], the common good[72], stewardship[73], and equality[74].

We must decide that one or more of these concepts should anchor our principles and form our Northstar, our direction to travel in. The reason for agreeing on the principle(s) is that collectively, we commit to a direction of travel to reach a better place. We state our principles as an ambition, goal or target to allow us to understand, manage and control uncertainty, using a risk framework. The risk framework frames or bounds the risks that we are prepared to take. The risk framework enables us to define rules to get to our known outcomes. We implement the rules to create controls using regulations, codes and standards. Our risk frameworks use tools to identify, measure, manage, monitor and report on the risk, the delta in risk, and compliance with the rules. Whilst all is good, we use the risk framework to create more rules and better framing and boundaries, in turn creating better outcomes. However, when the desired outcomes are not being created, we revert to our principles, consult our Northstar, and take new knowledge to refine/ redefine the risk that we are prepared to take.

Data introduces new principle problems!

Having established this framework, the idea is to apply this to data. We have an abundance of rules and regulations, and as many opinions on what we are trying to achieve with data. However, we don't appear to have an agreed risk framework for data at any level; individual, company, society, national or global. This is not a bill of rights, this is "what do we think is the Northstar for data, and on what principle should data be used?" How do these principles help us agree on risks, and will our existing rules help or hinder us?

> *"What do we think is the Northstar for data and on what principle should data be used?" How do these principles help us agree on risks, and will our existing rules help or hinder us?*

The question is, how do our principles change when the underlying fabric of what is possible changes? The world we originally designed for was physical; it is now digital-first. Now that we are becoming aware that the fabric of our world has changed, where next? For example, Lexis is the legal system database. With a case in mind, you can use this tool to uncover previous judgments and specific cases to inform your thinking.

However, this database is built on human and physical-first principles. Any digital judgements in this database are still predicated on the old frameworks. So, what is its value when the very fabric of all those judgements changes? Do we use it to slow us down, and prevent adoption of the new?

Time to unpack this.

Physical-world first (framed as AD 00 - 2010)

Classical thinking (western capital civilisation philosophy) defined values and principles which created policies, norms and rules. Today's policy is governed by people and processes. To improve our thinking we can look to history and can call on millennia of thought and wisdom. We create norms from what is trending/ leading as a philosophy.

In a physical and human-first world, we have multiple ways to position ourselves. We can start with the creation of a market, followed by norms, followed by doctrine/ architecture - in turn, creating law and regulations. OR we can start with norms, followed by doctrine/ architecture, followed by market-creating law.

Without our common and accepted beliefs, our physical world would not work. Law, money and rights are not real – they are command and control schema, underpinned by shared beliefs.

Our created norms are based on our experience with collective beliefs. We succeed by managing our appetite for risk.

Digital-world first (framed as AD 2020 - MMMCCX)

People in companies rather than people in government form the new norms, as companies have the capital to avoid rules and regulations. The most powerful companies are forming new rules to suit themselves. Companies possess the users, and accompanying data, to mould norms – behaviour can be directed, companies can set their own rules. Doctrine/ architecture creates the market, forming norms, and the law protects those who control the market. Policy can create rules, but it has no idea how rules are implemented or governed, as the companies increase complexity and reduce visibility of data. There are few signs of visible "core" human values, indeed, there are no shared and visible data principles.

The companies automate; the decisions become automated; the machine defines the rules, and changes the risk model. We are heading to the unknown and unimagined, as we have no core data principles.

For example: our news and media have changed models. Previously, the editor used their control to meet the demand of an audience willing to pay to have content orchestrated to their preferences. As advertising became important, content mirrored advertising preferences; editorial became the advertising, and advertising the content.

Digital tools created clicks that created the new model – anything that drives clicks, works. The fabric of news and media changed from physical to digital, and in doing so, lost the principles and rules of the physical-first world to a digital-first world that has not yet agreed on principles for data use.

Data is Data

In the next chapter, Data is Data[75], I explore what data is, my definition of data and my references.

Imagine looking at this framework of "principles, rules and risk" within the industries and sectors seeking to re-define, re-imagine and create new ways for people to manage the digital representations of themselves, with dignity. How would their data and privacy be presented?

With data (privacy, protection, use, collection) we have an abundance of rules and regulations, and as many opinions on what we should be trying to achieve with those rules and regulations. We appear to be missing an agreed risk framework for individuals, companies and societies (national and global).

These stated principles[76] are set out in Article 5[77] of the GDPR (General Data Protection Regulation) rules:

- Lawfulness, fairness and transparency
- Purpose limitation
- Data minimisation
- Accuracy
- Storage limitation
- Integrity and confidentiality (security)
- Accountability

We know they are called "Principles" by the framing of the heading in Article 5, however, if we read them critically, are these actually principles, values or rules? Consider, are these principles boundaries, stewardship ideals or a bit of a mashup? For example, to get around "Purpose Limitation," terms and conditions become as wide as possible so that all and or any use is possible. "Data minimisation" is only possible if you know exactly what data you want to gather, which is rarely the case if you are a data platform.

If a principle of The European Union is to ensure the free "movement / mobility" of people, goods, services and capital within the union (the "four freedoms"), do data identity ideals and GDPR align?

Before considering the "regulation" of Big Tech, we should ask - should they exist? Surely no one entity should have that much power[78] and control over people's data and ability to transact?

However, the current framing of Big Tech as acceptable won't create rules that actually move towards ending the current hegemony, but rather just seek to regulate it as is. If we include open APIs and the increasing level of data mobility, portability and sharing[79], whose "rules or principles" should be adopted?

As previously discussed, how do your principles change when the underlying fabric of what is possible changes? The entire privacy framework, as in the US today, is based on early 1970s reports written in the United States to address concerns over mass state databases that were proposed in the mid-late 1960s, and the growing data broker industry that was sending people unrequested catalogues. It doesn't account for the world we live in now, where "everyone" has a little computer in their pocket. Alas, in my opinion, GDPR is not much better than rules with no truly human-based core principles.

Conclusion

We appear to have outdated "principles" driving rules in a digital-first world. Our commercial world is now dominated by companies setting their own norms, without reference to any widely agreed-upon values.

The downside of big tech gaining so much power is that they are actually seen by those in government as equivalent to nation-states, and it is telling. Right now, we need historians, anthropologists, ontologists, psychologists, data scientists and regular everyday people, who are the users, to be able to close the loop between the rules we have, the risk frameworks we manage, and the principles that we should be aiming for.

Take away

- How are we checking that our rules are aligned to our principles?
- How are we checking our principles?
- Is our risk framework able to adapt to new principles, and changes in rules?
- How do we test that the rules that define and constrain can create better outcomes?

Chapter 7

Data; evidence and proof

3 part chapter

Part one: Data is data

Part two: Does data have purpose?

Part three: Wisdom is nothing more than new data. Wisdom is definitely not a summit

Chapter 7 - Part one

Data is data

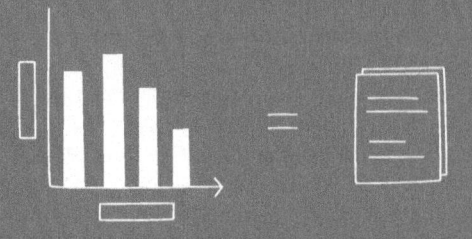

Data is not oil, gold, labour, fire, or sunshine. "Data is data", and because we don't understand its complexity, we keep creating bad analogies. This chapter explores what data truly is.

Data is not what we think it is

Words, in general, are a creative, symbolic, linguistic invention, through which people invoke concepts and meanings that are flexible, enabling us to shortcut detailed explanations. A dog is also a mammal, it barks, is furry, has four legs, teeth, etc. However, because words are a shortcut, they often lack relational context that adds meaning. Words are themselves "data", which requires the addition of meaning, derived from context, to inform the listener. In other words, to become information.

For example - love can mean or be interpreted to mean many different things, depending on context and relationship. The 2019 update to the New Oxford Dictionary brings in the words *agender* and *intersexual* to better define, and enable more nuanced conversations about, sexuality and gender identity. Better words help us to avoid conflict and confrontation.

Words allow us to explore and debate wider and deeper concepts. Their misunderstanding can lead to fights, war, turmoil and anger; or innovation, problem solving and creativity. Sometimes we don't have a word for something, and therefore must spend time using metaphors and adding context to our speech. An interesting question is: how did we describe competition before the word "competition"? In 1996, Nicholas Negroponte wrote a book titled "Being Digital[80]". In the book, he spends an entire chapter explaining broadband, another explaining social media, another on defining e-commerce. Historically, defining things took up a lot of our time.

Humans process words depending upon a rich tapestry of context, relationships, mood, as well as how it was said, when it was said, and by whom. To make sense of words individually, we interpret combinations of words using our own bias. This abstract view of sense-making comes from, and is baked into, our experiences and the order and weight we give to such experiences. Shakespeare's plays are all written using the same 26 alphabet letters. Knowing the symbols and even the words does not allow easy access to meaning - and at best, reading is a starting point in trying to determine Shakespeare's message.

Economics, biology, physics, psychology, and maths have all created their own language and words to explain the order of things. This has allowed us to construct better explanations and also create value, wealth and prosperity. However, in economics, for example, the order given to words is based on the general concepts of scarcity and abundance, and the equations of supply and demand. Therefore, the established words possess certain limitations and assumptions, which means that they may not work well to describe new models, theories or markets. Faced with new ideas, the words and descriptions break down.

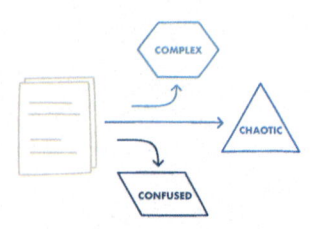

Figure 1: Data is not what it seems

The reason for this long introduction and context is to make the point that we lack words to describe the new activities, models and functions of a **data-driven digital world**. Our current vocabulary may constrain and slow us down, because of some of the ambiguities inherent in the words we currently use. For example, consider the application of the word identity[81]: as in "name"; identity as in "provider"; and identity used to mean "access" - context and relationship matter. Consider the internet descriptor language we commonly use. We say there are *sites, domains* and *locations*, that we *visit* and *browse*; so framing the Internet as real estate, which is something we can relate to. When we speak of *pages* that we *author, publish* and *syndicate*, we are framing the Web as a publishing system. When we speak of *content*, consisting of *packets* that we *move, upload, download* and *store* with *addresses*, we're framing the underlying infrastructure as freight, moving between storage facilities. Analogies such as these inevitably have their limitations.

The word "data" poses a particular problem, as it is a word that we want to constrain by describing with context and relationships, but "data" does not comply with the same boundaries or constraints as other words. As much as we would like to explain data and its functions with a metaphor or analogy, it is unique. Data is closer to the discovery of a new core element for the periodic table; a new energy concept for quantum that allows us to understand something we could not previously explain; or a new model for dark matter.

Every model we use to explain data fails. Data is not oil, we don't mine or refine it. Data is not gold; there is more data than there are atoms in the universe. Data is not labour; it does not begin and end. Generally, data is not a commodity. Commodities, at least of the sort that get bought and sold in stores and in commodities markets, are both rivalrous[82] and excludable[83] by nature. Data is, by its nature, non-rivalrous and non-excludable.

> **The simple fact is that you cannot declare ownership of data (though many people try), you cannot control it, and you lose nothing when you copy it. It is why data is just that - data.**

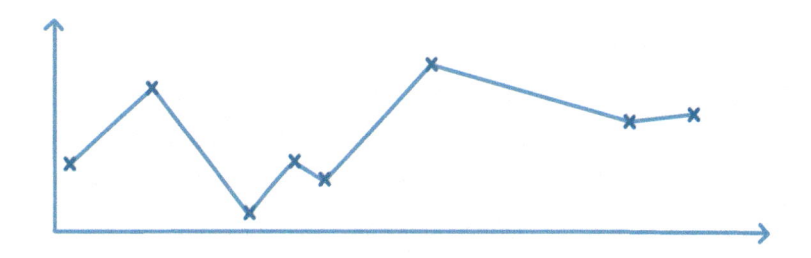

Metaphorical framing

In fact, by their very design, all metaphors are wrong. For example, time is not money - but we use money to frame our understanding of time. That's why we save it, spend it, waste it, invest it and put it aside. Likewise, life is not travel; yet birth is arrival, death is departure, choices are crossroads, we get stuck in a rut, lost in the woods, get back on track, and so on.

This metaphorical framing makes full sense to us as humans, because our experiences of time and life are very much ones of valuable commodities (time as money) and movement (life as travel). As explored in the "Mind is Flat[84]" by Nick Chater, our brains are built to create and make sense of the world: we need metaphors to make the initial jump, but then the words themselves move us forward.

> However, the words and metaphors we use for the Internet, the Web and Data insult us all, and that's a problem. Our digital world is too radically new and different to be fully conceptualised, understood, explained and honoured by the metaphors we apply to them. They are limited by words that have the wrong meaning - so, it is time to build a new vocabulary!

We talk about data as a commodity, just as we talk about time. But while our experience of time is of a finite non-thing, our experience of data is something like the Sorcerer's Apprentice's experience of magic: it gets way out of control.

Joyce Searls points out that our experience in the Web is one of "no gravity[85]" (because the Internet isn't a place, and we are incorporeal chimeras to each other there: damn fine ghosts or holograms, but not physically real), and of no distance. She also thinks we'll adapt to those conditions, but that it's still too early to predict with full confidence, from our experiences so far.

Creating value from data requires an entirely new vocabulary to prevent a breakdown of understanding. Just like when we talk about "data as oil", definitions of *data storage, data consent, data analysis*, and more, fall apart when put into different contexts and relationships. As an example, *data storage* is not the same now as it was with the economic model we had for the storage of documents in 1980. By 2018, digital data storage has a relationship and content to security, access, rights, liability, control, sharing, as well as conflicting national compliance laws and privacy changes. However, we continue to use dated economic framing, thinking and words to describe these new data functions, which then fail.

There is a wider point to be made around data storage: is storing data useful or useless? Is data as useful or as useless as a bad memory that stops a person from falling in love, taking a promotion or starting their own business? These metaphors add depth to conversation and demonstrate how our words fall apart all too quickly.

As Doc Searls[86] puts it *"We are now digital as well as physical beings, and our habitat as digital beings is very new, strange and has no history, so we are forming new human experiences, even though we live in a digital world almost as much as we live in the natural world".*

From the 10th to the 21st century, our thinking built a vocabulary that was based on an economic model that existed in the here and now; physical and limited by space and time. Relationships and formulas were discovered, explained and modelled. In our new data-driven world, the vocabularies that describe the physical are holding us back, as we are having to explain more and more of the context of and relationships between words to make sense. If the objective value of a word is to create a shortcut, using the wrong words means we waste more time explaining than we can spend creating. Our new data-driven world needs new words to describe the new functions. This world is not constrained by established vocabulary that we have developed to describe the relationship between time and space (we will probably discover that vocabulary to be limited, anyway!). Our new data-driven world is messy, interwound, interconnected, interdependent, driven, causal, necessitates immediacy, and is relationship and feedback driven.

Our history and experience has provided context and relevance to words, which has become baked into our laws. In a data-driven world, "trust" has new meanings where new dependent relationships and contexts change our understanding. The MIT study that led to the "Privacy Paradox[87]" is a good example of how the word "privacy" does not work when we talk about data. Do people just want privacy to avoid exploitation and danger, or to mitigate their sense of vulnerability?

Or, are people willing to trade "privacy" in order for the control to manipulate their data and live out their life fantasies in a digital world? Are people so addicted to the control they have in shaping their digital lives, that they are only concerned that a privacy, security breach or fraud brings them back to their analogue life? A person (maybe) owns their body, mind and thoughts, but do they truly own their data?

Let's explore one idea that needs a concise word, as a starter. "Data ownership". If we had a better word that describes the context and relationships associated with data ownership, we could save pages of debate. Can you actually own data? It would be simple if the answer was yes, whilst the reality is no; however, you can own the machine and software that stores data, and different players do have different rights to the data.

In fact, the non-rivalrous nature of data wreaks havoc with modern notions of ownership. The Romans had a much subtler understanding of the nuances of "ownership", when they created separate legal rights and processes for usus, fructus and abusus[88].

In Roman times, *Usus* (use) was the right to use or enjoy a thing directly, without altering it. For example, to walk on a piece of land or eat a fig from a fig tree. *Fructus* (fruit, in a figurative sense) was the right to derive profit from a thing possessed: for instance, by selling crops (but not the land on which they were produced), taxing for entry, etc. Finally, *abusus* (literally translated as abuse) was the right to alienate the thing possessed, either by consuming or destroying it, or by transferring it to someone else (e.g. sale, exchange, gift). When applied to territory, these notions of *usus, fructus* and *abusus* imply not strictly "private property", but a notion that different rights apply inside and outside clearly delineated boundaries.

When the 18th-century constitutionalist William Blackstone observed that an Englishman's home was his castle, he wasn't talking about absolute rights of private property. Rather, he was talking about Englishmen defending a piece of territory in which they were safe. Englishmen didn't just have their castles, they also shared the fruits and benefits of commons[89], public rights of way[90], and so on. Each of these different territories had specific rules and rights associated with them. In contrast to this subtle ecosystem of rights and responsibilities, Blackstone characterised modern notions of private property as the "sole and despotic dominion, which one man claims and exercises over the external things of the world, in total exclusion of the right to any other individual in the universe".

In a new data-driven age, we need to establish a new concept within digital and data spheres, that builds appropriate boundaries; each with their own rules, rights and responsibilities. Critically, individuals' rights to *usus, fructus*, as well as *abusus*, in relation to their own data, need to be clearly delineated. This is very different to current debates about "control", virtually all of which relate to individuals trying to control what other parties do with their data - rather than having the right and ability to use their own data, for their own purposes.

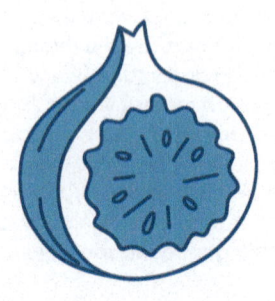

As discussed earlier, "data" itself is also a problematic word; and by extension, so is the entire emerging world of cryptocurrency. "Data" has many different definitions (a quick search gives well over 50 to play with), and individual labels and biases. We can be specifically clear about what we are talking about with data types - as long as a verb is included. Flat, big, meta, real-time, old, static, new, current, statistical, empirical, computer, binary, linked, etc. However, not all "data" is created equal, and as such, data is contextual to where value may lie, which can be either good for humanity, or good for the value of the players who are able to exploit it. As yet, we have not been able to add context to our definitions of data: including issues such as rights, ownership, providence, trust, privacy, security, faithfulness, and correctness.

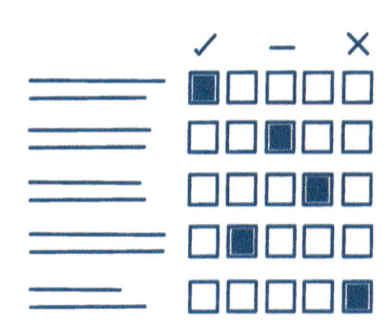

Is there a similar problem elsewhere that provides precedent?

Whilst risk, beauty or compassion are useful thought experiments when attempting to answer this question, they lack the direct linkage to value creation that data provides. Data is data!

From Wikipedia: *Risk is the possibility of losing something of value. Values (such as physical health[91], social status[92], emotional wellbeing, or financial wealth) can be gained or lost when taking risk resulting from a given action or inaction, foreseen or unforeseen (planned or not planned). Risk can also be defined as the intentional interaction with uncertainty[93]. Uncertainty is a potential, unpredictable, and uncontrollable outcome; risk is a consequence of action taken in spite of uncertainty.*

It is possible that "risk" could be helpful as a conceptual framework, as it has some properties similar to "data". Risk cannot be owned or held physically (but it can be accounted for); it cannot be controlled or touched; it changes continually; it has no value in of itself; it cannot be weighed or measured in the real world; it can be passed, sold and assigned, but cannot be "copied"; we can only describe potential outcomes, and assign a risk measure. Risk is totally subjective and we all make different judgments regarding the severity and probability of any and all risks. All human endeavour carries risk, but some can be defined as being much riskier than others, depending on the lens in which it is viewed.

So what...

Creating new words may not happen, but there are companies that are solving and delivering solutions in our new data-driven world, and have ideas of privacy, consent, rights, ownership, sharing, and storage as core functions. However, words become commonplace in our vocabulary over time: "Hoover" became a generic name for a function, "Google" for search, "Text" for messaging, and there are many more examples.

Should we (the digital community) start to adopt names of companies, which have the single function of delivering context in this new data-driven world, to allow us to describe data functions in a clear and crisp way?

Would such adoption get us closer to value creation, growth and fun a whole lot quicker? Would we remove the need for using different words with the same core meaning, that slow us from agreeing on a solution and moving forwards?

Extending this to AI — given that AI needs data

As a final thought, do the lack of current descriptors for data provide a rationale as to why AI will be slower to in adoption than perhaps the technology would enable? Is the timing of its development such that we will spend too much time debating words that cannot describe the concepts, and therefore, cannot provide the assurance or governance that is required for its adoption?

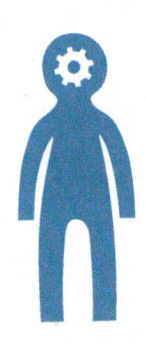

Chapter 7 - Part two

Does data have a purpose?

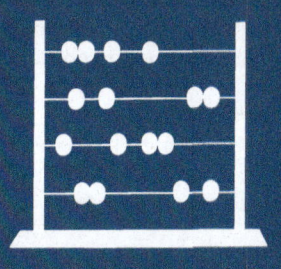

If the purpose of data is "to share state", then the two essential characteristics data must have are rights and attestation. As data becomes information (knowing state), knowledge (patterns of states), insight (context in states), and wisdom, these characteristics of rights and attestation matter even more.

As we desire better data-led decisions, we should be aware that we can easily ask the wrong questions of our datasets. Without understanding the purpose of the dataset on which we are basing decisions and judgements, it is easy to reach answers that are not actually found in the data we have. How can we understand if our Northstar (and with it, our direction and decisions) is a good one? This is an important topic to consider as we focus on improving governance and oversight in a data-led world.

The first part of this chapter was Data is Data[94]. It was a kickback at the analogies that data can be compared to oil, gold, labour, sunlight - it cannot. Data is unique; it has unique characteristics. This first part concluded that the word "Data" is also part of the problem - we should instead think of data as if discovering a new element with unique characteristics.

Data is a word, and it is part of the problem. Data doesn't have meaning or shape, and data will not have meaning unless we can give it context.

As Theodora Lau[95] eloquently put it: if her kiddo gets 10 points in a test today (data as a state), the number 10 has no meaning, unless we also say that she scored 10 points out of 10 in the test today (data as information). And even then, we still need to explain the type of test (data as knowledge) and what to do next or how to improve (data as insights). Each of these is a "data" point, and yet we do not differentiate the use of the word "data" in each of these contexts.

Data's most fundamental representation is "state" where it represents the particular condition something is in at a specific time. I love Hugh Macleod's[96] work (@gapingvoid) - the representation below shows that *information* is knowing that there are different "states" (on/off). *Knowledge* is finding patterns and connections between those states. *Insight* knows which comparisons are useful. *Wisdom* is the journey from one state to another. We live in the hope that the data we have will have a significant *impact*.

Figure 1: Gapingvoid's representation of different uses of data

For a while, the data community has rested on two key characteristics of data: non-rivalrous *(which wreaks havoc with our current understanding of ownership)* and non-fungible *(which is true, if you assume that data carries information)*. Whilst these are both accurate observations; they are not that good as universal characteristics.

Non-rivalrous. Economists call an item that can only be used by one person at a time as "rivalrous." Money and capital are rivalrous. Data is non-rivalrous, as a single item of data can simultaneously fuel multiple algorithms, analytics, and applications. This is, however, not strictly true. Numerous perfect copies of "data" can be used simultaneously, because the marginal cost of reproduction and sharing is zero.

Non-fungible. When you can substitute one item for another, they are said to be fungible. One sovereign bill can be replaced for another sovereign bill of the same value; one barrel of oil is the same as the next. So the thinking goes that data is non-fungible and cannot be substituted because it carries information. However, if your view is that data carries "state" *(the particular condition that something is in at a specific time)*, then data is fungible. Higher-level ideals of data types, which are processed (information, knowledge, insights), are increasingly non-fungible.

Money as a framework to explore the purpose of data

Sovereign currency (FIAT[97]), for our purposes, "money", has two essential characteristics. It is rivalrous and fungible. Without these foundational characteristics, money cannot fulfil its original purpose (though it has many others now) as a trusted exchange medium.

Money removes the former necessity of a direct barter, where equal value had to be established, and the two or more parties had to meet for an exchange. What is interesting is that there are alternatives to FIAT which exploit other properties. Because of fraud, we have to have security features, and there is a race to build the most secure wall.

121

Figure 2: Fungible, non-fungible, rivalrous, and non-rivalrous currencies

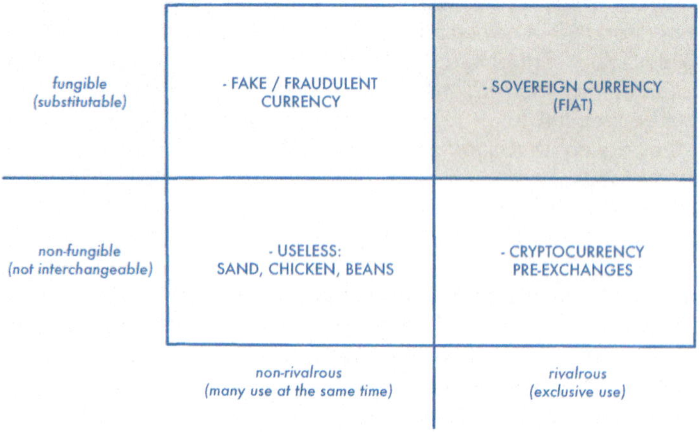

fungible (substitutable)	- FAKE / FRAUDULENT CURRENCY	- SOVEREIGN CURRENCY (FIAT)
non-fungible (not interchangeable)	- USELESS: SAND, CHICKEN, BEANS	- CRYPTOCURRENCY PRE-EXCHANGES
	non-rivalrous (many use at the same time)	rivalrous (exclusive use)

[Just as a side note - money is an abstraction, and part of the rationale for the balance sheet was to try to connect this abstraction back to real things. I am not sure that this works any more]

Revising the matrix "what problem is to be solved?"

Adding these other options of exchange onto the matrix, we have a different way to frame the problems that each type of currency offers as a method of exchange mechanism. This is presented in the chart below. Sand and beans can be used, but they provide a messy tool compared to a sovereign currency. Crypto works, and it solves the problem - but without exchange to other currencies, it has fundamental limits.

Figure 3: Advantages and disadvantages of currencies

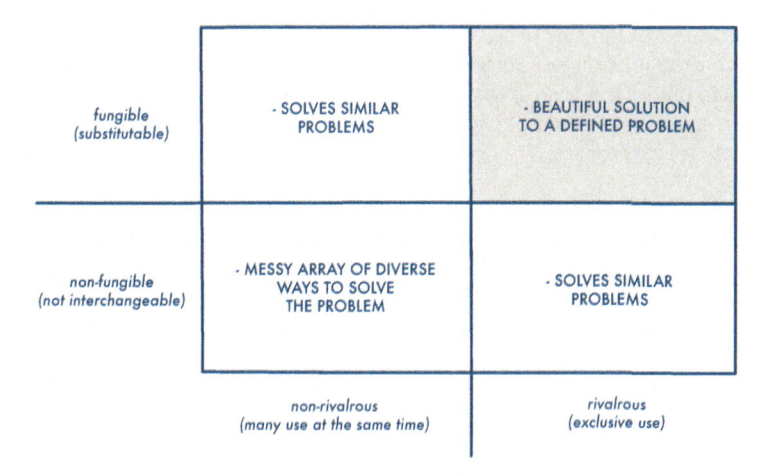

	non-rivalrous (many use at the same time)	rivalrous (exclusive use)
fungible (substitutable)	- SOLVES SIMILAR PROBLEMS	- BEAUTIFUL SOLUTION TO A DEFINED PROBLEM
non-fungible (not interchangeable)	- MESSY ARRAY OF DIVERSE WAYS TO SOLVE THE PROBLEM	- SOLVES SIMILAR PROBLEMS

If we now add digital data and other aspects of our world onto the matrix, we have an entirely different perspective. We all share gravity and sunsets, and broadcast TV/ radio on electromagnetic waves. However, only one atom can be used at a time, and that atom is non-interchangeable (to get the same outcome.)

The point here is that digital data is not in the same quadrant as sovereign currency, and electrons, fungible and rivalrous, would be a beautiful solution. Using the broadest definition of data, as a "state"; chemicals, atoms, gravity, and electrons have state, and therefore are also data. To be clear, we will now use digital data to define our focus, not all data.

Figure 4: Imagining different currencies

	non-rivalrous (many use at the same time)	rivalrous (exclusive use)
fungible (substitutable)	- ELECTROMAGNETISM - SUNSETS - GRAVITY - SAME ELEMENT	- SOVEREIGN CURRENCY (FIAT) - ELECTRONS - QUANTUM PARTICLES
non-fungible (not interchangeable)	- DIGITAL DATA	- CHEMICAL REACTION - ATOMS

These updates to the matrix highlight that data is non-rivalrous and non-fungible, and that these characteristics make it unclear which problems digital data is solving. We see this all the time in the digital data market, as we cannot agree on what "data" is - it is messy.

The question for us as a digital data community is "what are the axes [characteristics] that place digital data in the top corner of a matrix?". This quadrant is where digital data is a beautiful solution to a defined problem, given that digital data is at its core is "knowing state." I explored this question on a call with Scott David[98], and we ended up resting on "**Rights**" and "**Attestation**" as the two axes.

Rights, in this context, mean that you have gained principles of entitlement to the data from the Parties (individual or group, defined as one entity for legal purposes). What and how those rights were acquired is not of interest; all that matters is that you have the rights needed to do what you need to do.

Attestation, in this context, is the evidence or proof of something. It means that you know what you have is true and that you can prove the state exists. How you do this is not the point; rather, you know it is provable.

Figure 5: Rights and attestation in data

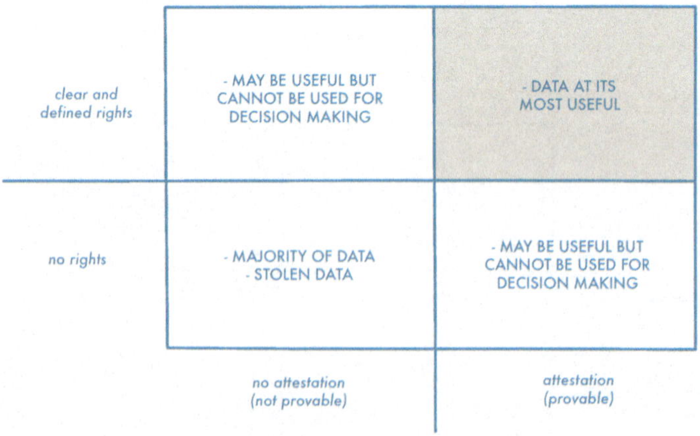

	no attestation (not provable)	attestation (provable)
clear and defined rights	- MAY BE USEFUL BUT CANNOT BE USED FOR DECISION MAKING	- DATA AT ITS MOST USEFUL
no rights	- MAJORITY OF DATA - STOLEN DATA	- MAY BE USEFUL BUT CANNOT BE USED FOR DECISION MAKING

As we saw with the money example, data will never have these characteristics (rights and attestation) exclusively; but when it has them, data is at its most purposeful. Without attestation, the data you have is compromised, and any conclusions you reach may not be true or real. We must continuously test both our assumptions and the attestation of our digital data. "Rights" are different, as these are not correlated with data quality – but, rights may help resolve ownership issues. A business built without adequate rights to the data they are using is not stable or sustainable. How and if those rights were obtained ethically are matters to be investigated. Interestingly, these characteristics (rights and attestation) would readily fit into existing risk and audit frameworks.

I have a specific focus on ESG, sustainability, data for decision making, and better data for sharing. Given that most comparative ESG data is from public reports (creative commons, or free of rights), it is essential to note that there is a break in the attestation of this data. Currently, ESG data is sourced from the least useful data bucket for decision making, but is the dataset that we are using to make critical investment decisions. This oversight is something that we must address.

In summary:

If the purpose of data is "to share state" then the two essential characteristics data must have are rights and attestation. Further, as data becomes information (knowing state), knowledge (patterns of states), insight (context in states) and wisdom, these characteristics of rights and attestation matter even more. If you are making decisions using data that you don't know is true, or have the rights to use, this becomes dangerous.

As a side note, there are plenty of technologies and processes to enable us to know if the state is true (as in correct - not truth); if the state sensing is working; the level of accuracy; if the state at both ends has the same representation (providence/ lineage); if it is secure; if we can gain information from it; if we can combine datasets; and what the ontology of the data is. But these are not fundamental characteristics - they are supportive and ensure we have a vibrant ecosystem of digital data.

I am sure there are other labels for such a matrix and I am interested in feedback, views, thoughts and opinions. Making Fire!

Chapter 7 - Part three

Wisdom is nothing more than new data. Wisdom is definitely not a summit

You may often hear of a journey that begins with data acquisition and ends in the accumulation of wisdom (established knowledge, based on experience). In these stories, we imagine wisdom as the summit, something to aspire to. But wisdom itself is just another data point that needs to be tested.

There is undoubtedly less wisdom than there is data, but that does not mean anything more than when using the metric of volume, there will be more data than wisdom.

We do love the shape of a triangle; the summit, or pinnacle. We love to imagine that wisdom has more value than data, that somehow, it is more noble and worthy - as only a few will obtain true wisdom. The idea being if I obtain it, I will sit at the top of the tree.

Figure 1: Our perceived journey from data to wisdom

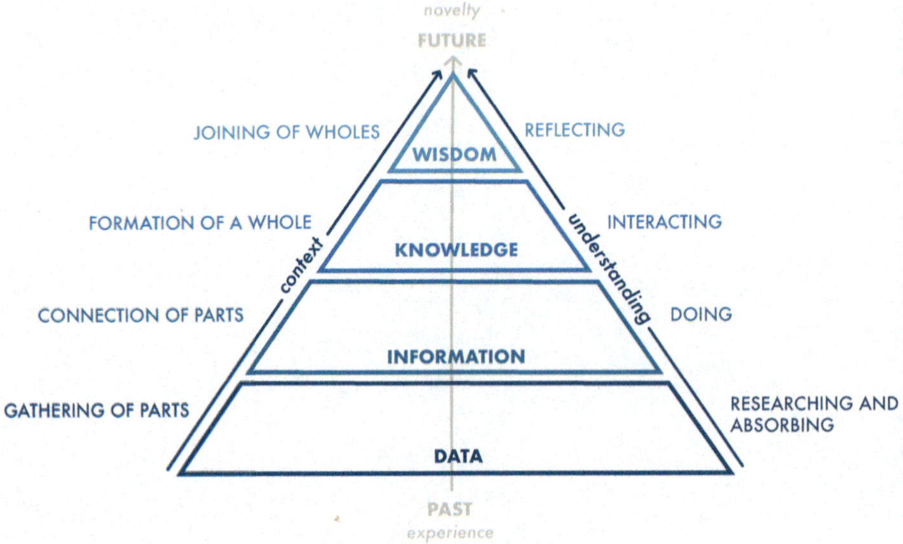

novelty
FUTURE

JOINING OF WHOLES — WISDOM — REFLECTING

FORMATION OF A WHOLE — KNOWLEDGE — INTERACTING

context / understanding

CONNECTION OF PARTS — INFORMATION — DOING

GATHERING OF PARTS — DATA — RESEARCHING AND ABSORBING

PAST
experience

Let's unpack this thinking

Here we are starting with Maslow's Hierarchy of needs, and his 1943 paper "A Theory of Human Motivation", which presents a theory for motivation. Maslow's hierarchy of needs was originally proposed as a framework, enabling the study of how humans intrinsically partake in behavioural motivation. Interestingly, he did not draw a triangle, but a square block with several rectangle layers.

"Hierarchy" came from the description of the pattern through which human motivations generally move, towards progression and achievement. We later converted the square to a triangle for use as a tool to model motivation, implying that we should aim for the top. However, as shown below, the view of self-actualization as a peak is a very Western view of the world, and does not align with all people and their beliefs.

Figure 2: Maslow's hierarchy of needs (informed by blackfoot nations (ALTA))

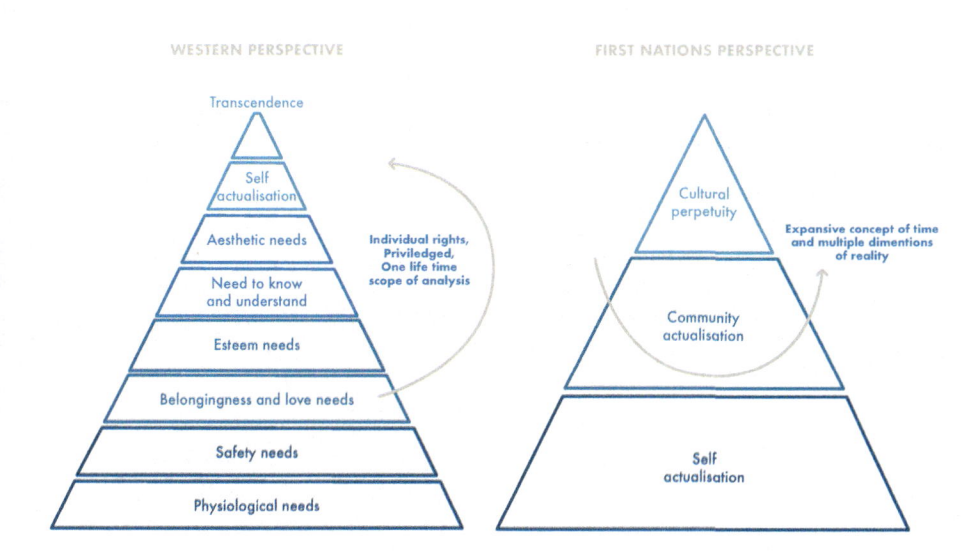

WESTERN PERSPECTIVE

- Transcendence
- Self actualisation
- Aesthetic needs
- Need to know and understand
- Esteem needs
- Belongingness and love needs
- Safety needs
- Physiological needs

Individual rights, Priviledged, One life time scope of analysis

FIRST NATIONS PERSPECTIVE

- Cultural perpetuity
- Community actualisation
- Self actualisation

Expansive concept of time and multiple dimentions of reality

The lesson here is that triangles are very biassed in terms of what they want you to think. A triangle with a point, like a mountain summit, is something to reach the top of.

However, I have been to the summit of a few high mountains (over 6,000m/ 20,000ft) and still, there are always more mountains to climb, and there are way more peaks than days in my life. Ultimately, reaching the top is only a moment in time.

The triangle framing hinders our thinking; let's question this framing

Back to the conventional wisdom that is built on the data triangle

I love the story of the Judgement of Solomon[99]. It is a story from the Bible, in which King Solomon of Israel ruled between two women, both claiming to be the mother of a child. Solomon revealed their true feelings and relationship to the child by suggesting to cut the baby in two, with each woman to receive half. With this strategy, he was able to discern the non-mother as the woman who entirely approved of this proposal, while the actual mother begged that the sword might be sheathed and the child committed to the care of her rival. Some consider this approach to justice an archetypal[100] example of an impartial judge displaying wisdom in making a ruling.

I was taught that this is wisdom - that it would be good to be as wise as King Solomon. However, I now realise there is a flaw in this wisdom. If you think about it, it can only be wise once. There is a queue of women, all who have disputes over who owns the child. Up steps the first case. Solomon announces to cut the baby in half. We know the story.

The next pair of women step forward. They have heard and seen the story; both women now declare that the baby should not be harmed. The wisdom is lost, as there is new data. Solomon must quickly find a new way to determine who is the mother - maybe he will ask a trusted source.

As more pairs step forward, one by one, with more and more scenarios at hand, there is now a game of lies and falsehoods, with the game outcome to hold the baby. Each case is not generating more wisdom, is it really just more data.

Over time, thinking has progressed on the non-linear building of wisdom - but perhaps we need to refine this thinking further. As we gain insights from data, it is only more data. As we use the insights from data in decisions, it is only more data. As we model complexity and determine the delta between our model and reality, it is only more data. The following figure is from Carpenter's 2008 paper[101] on Hierarchies of Understanding.

Figure 3: Carpenter's paper on Hierarchies of Understanding, 2008

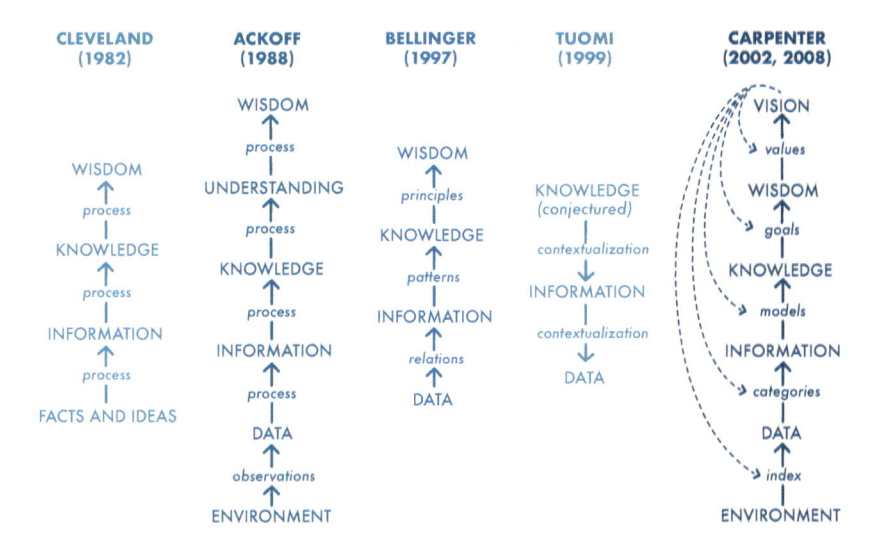

CLEVELAND (1982)	ACKOFF (1988)	BELLINGER (1997)	TUOMI (1999)	CARPENTER (2002, 2008)
WISDOM ↑ process ↑ KNOWLEDGE ↑ process ↑ INFORMATION ↑ process ↑ FACTS AND IDEAS	WISDOM ↑ process ↑ UNDERSTANDING ↑ process ↑ KNOWLEDGE ↑ process ↑ INFORMATION ↑ process ↑ DATA ↑ observations ↑ ENVIRONMENT	WISDOM ↑ principles ↑ KNOWLEDGE ↑ patterns ↑ INFORMATION ↑ relations ↑ DATA	KNOWLEDGE (conjectured) ↓ contextualization ↓ INFORMATION ↓ contextualization ↓ DATA	VISION ⤳ values ↓ WISDOM ⤳ goals ↓ KNOWLEDGE ⤳ models ↓ INFORMATION ⤳ categories ↓ DATA ⤳ index ↓ ENVIRONMENT

Wisdom is just a shift register

In systems engineering, a shift register is a way of storing and recalling information. First In First Out (FIFO) and Last In First Out (LIFO) are two easy cases to explain. They are both methods of storing data in memory. Here, I am considering how we store and recall things.

In FIFO type memory the data that is stored first is removed first. It is like accessing the stack from below, with the order remaining the same. In LIFO type memory, the data that is stored last on the stack is removed first, i.e., to be stored, the data stacks on top of each other, and the order is reversed.

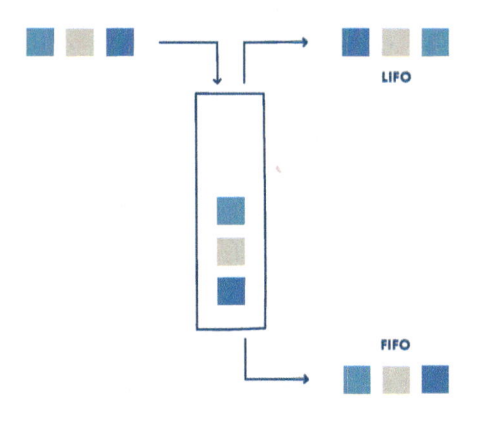

Figure 4: FIFO and FIFO data storage

There are also the First In, Last Out (FILO) and Last In, Last Out (LILO) methods of data storage.

Perhaps we should apply the triangle thinking around data to wisdom, and think of this process as a shift register.

We can take data from what we learn to help improve the whole cycle, rather than thinking that more data will simply create more wisdom. Old data and early wisdom should be placed in a deep place, which is harder to access (but not quite lost).

Figure 5: Different methods of storing and recalling information

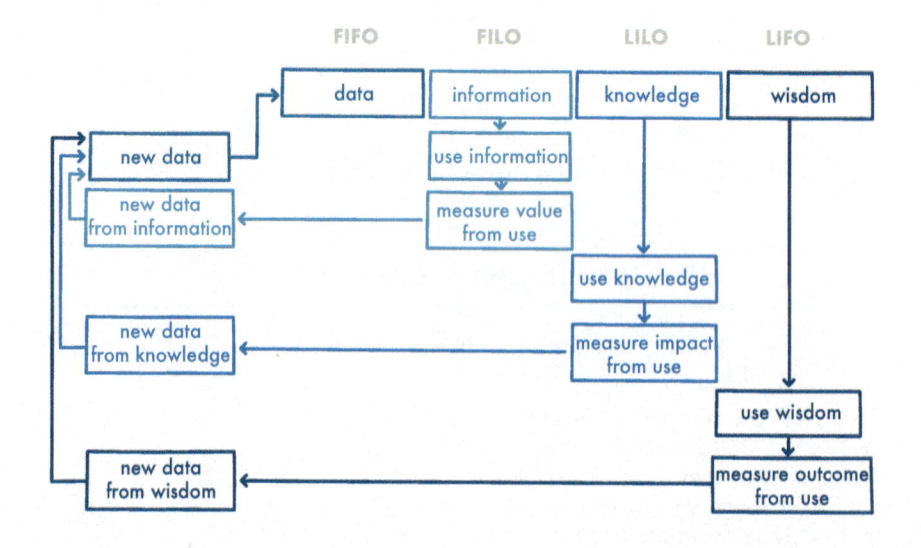

> **From this, we can see that...**

Data is First in, First out. You can easily recall what you just learned. It is not tested, checked or known to be true. It is why we all share things we find without knowing how truthful or biassed it is. This often causes us to share data that is not as accurate as we think it is.

Information is First In, Last out. This slows the immediacy of response and allows us to gather more data before we start to decide on our decision or action. It is a great way of improving quality. Once we have used this information, we can feed back on what value it created and determine if it is useful.

Knowledge is Last In, Last out. Again this slows the response further, to gather everything before determining if there is new knowledge, or just a new fact that does not change the overall analysis. Using this knowledge we can feed back on the impact it created, and therefore if it had the desired outcome, or what the delta is.

Wisdom is Last In, First Out. We reverse the order, using the most recent wisdom first. We measure the outcome from when wisdom was used, to learn if it worked - and also to adjust our decisions or actions the next time we get to use wisdom.

When we use information, knowledge or wisdom in decision making we will always have to balance feeling, intuition and facts. No matter how much data we have, on its own, it will not always lead to better decisions or better outcomes.

So perhaps wisdom is nothing more than new data, if we apply and measure its efficacy. Taking this forward as a concept, it means that we can focus on making better decisions and judgements without the burden of climbing a summit that does not exist.

Chapter 8

Data; choice, decisions and railroading

Three part chapter

Part one: Data for better decision structures - nature or nurture?

Part two: Data framing affects your perception of everything

Part three: Is the data presented to you enabling a real choice?

Chapter 8 - Part one

Data for better decision structures – nature or nurture?

This chapter explores why it is likely that if you adhere to a data philosophy/ ontology/ structure, you can only understand what that structure will shine a light on and enable you to see.

Data can guide and lead but cannot pick the direction

Figure 1: Scatted plot of observed and predicted attainment

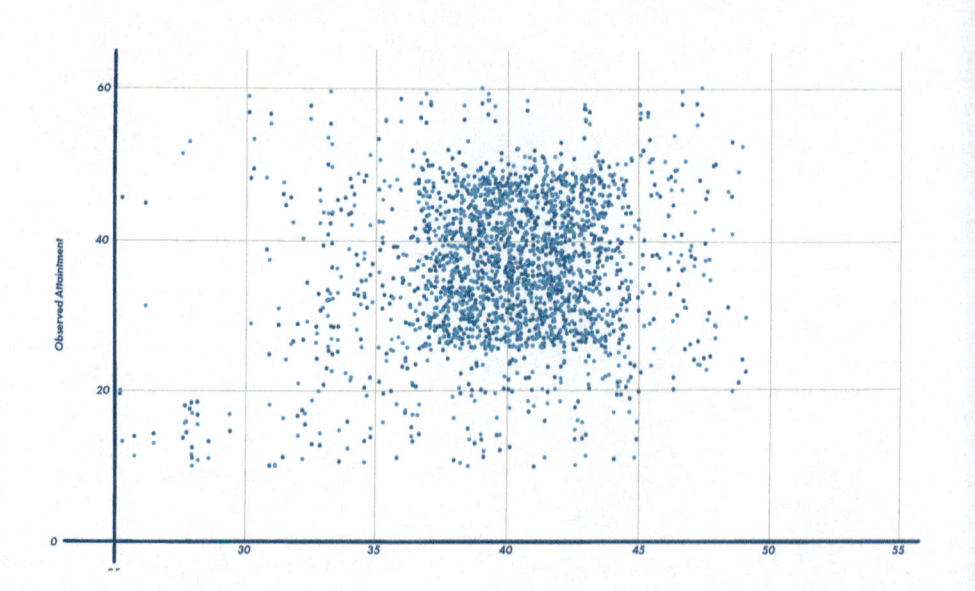

"Every" management student has had to answer the exam question: "Leadership/ management: nature or nurture? – discuss". It is a paradox from either side of the argument, the "logical" conclusion always highlights that the other has truth. The reality of leadership and management is that it is a complex adaptive system, and context enables your nature to emerge, and your nurturing to mature. This is important because we also know there is a link between strategy, styles (leadership) and business structures. In this chapter, we will unpack how your "nature or nurture" thinking structure affects outcomes of decision making. Your thinking structure is also a complex adaptive system; it is affected by your peers and customers' thinking, and your company's "culture of structure" thinking. BUT have you considered how your data structure and your data philosophy will have a direct and significant impact on those outcomes?

I'm aware that my neurodiversity package (severe dyslexia, mild high-functioning autism, ADHD) informs how I interrupt the world - my "biological cortex" and gut-brain axis structures process sensory data and memory uniquely. I cannot modify my mind or brain's basic structure any more than I could change my fingerprint, core DNA or the colour of my eyes; whilst I can play with my microbiome. These are essential parts of what makes me, me. My chemical and biological structures enable me to make sense of the world in my own unique way.

Communication (language, words, music, song, dance, art, sound, movement, gesture) enables us to share the senses we create from patterns around us, and align with others who share our experiences (our tribe). How we actually make sense (learn) is intensely debated, with one camp believing that language is our sense maker, assuming that we might observe patterns but cannot understand it without language. Otherwise, we make sense and then we create a language to communicate the insight we have gained. Irrespective, language allows us to both structure and navigate our space in the world and share our journey.

Our past is not easy to face up to

Why does this question matter? We all read, speak and write differently, we all understand differently, but we use commonly understood questions to clarify understanding and meaning. How we individually structure meaning is determined from the perspective we have been given (nature), what we have been taught (nurture) and what we align to (bias). Our structure is an ontology*. Imagine putting one person from each of our worlds' religions or faith groups into a room, but assume that no one can speak the same language. They would have nothing to agree or disagree on as there is no common structure (ontology) to enable debate.

---

* An ontology is "the set of things whose existence is acknowledged by a particular theory or system of thought" (The Oxford Companion to Philosophy).

For example, the word "evil" creates meaning for you as soon as you read it. Without a doubt, the nature of "evil" is a complex and nuanced area, too often glossed over in a rush to present or evaluate defences and theodicies. Let's unpack the word using the super book "[Making Evil][102]" by [Dr Julia Shaw][103]. Evil is an unavoidable part of life that we all encounter as we suffer in one sense or another, but what makes something "evil" is a matter of framing/ structure/ ontology. "Natural evil" is the pain and suffering that arises from the natural world's functioning or malfunctioning. "Moral evil" is the pain and suffering that results from conscious human action or inaction. It is evil where a person or people are to blame for the suffering that occurs; the crucial point here is the blameworthiness of the person at fault.

Moral evil, at its heart, results from the free choice of a moral agent. If we just look at the consequences, it is not always possible to tell whether moral evil has taken place or not, there are many mitigations. What is important is the degree of intention and consequence. However, if we compare death rates for natural evil (suffering) and moral evil (at its extreme, people killing people), the latter is a rounding error in the form of suffering in the world. The point here is that by framing the concept of "evil", I can create a structure for understanding. Critically, our existing structures are what frames our understanding.

Critically, our existing structures are what frames our understanding.

Structures are ontologies, which are philosophies.

To explore how our structures frame our understanding, we must first understand which ontologies make us human. When we look at the ontologies below, we can view ourselves as humans in many different ways.

Our framing, or how we structure something from the beginning, guides us to our conclusions.

Pick a different structure, and you get a different answer; the ontology creates the conclusion. It is likely that if you pick a specific philosophy/ ontology/ structure, you can only reach a conclusion that your framing will shine a light on or enable.

It is likely that if you pick a specific philosophy/ ontology/ structure, you can only reach a conclusion that your framing will shine a light on or enable.

Note: I have deliberately ignored the classical "all living things" ontology structure (insects, birds, fish, mammal, reptiles, plants). The point here is that your framing, or how you structure something from the beginning, guides you to your conclusions.

Figure 2: Different ontologies

Make up	Chemistry	Parts	Organs	Cells	Behaviour	Intelligence
Water Protein Fats Minerals Other	Oxygen Carbon Hydrogen Nitrogen Calcium Phosphorus Other	Head Eyes Ears Mouth Body Arms Legs	Skin Brain Liver Kidney Heart Stomach Intestine	Muscle Bacteria Erythrocytes Adipocytes Other	Social Anti-social Individual Team Shared	Language Writing Understanding Awareness Questions Consequences Imagination Creativity

This matters because all data has structure!

I continuously explore the future of the digital business, which is underpinned by data, privacy, consent and identity. In this book, chapter 7 included Data is Data, Does data have a purpose?, and Wisdom is nothing more than new data; whilst chapter 3 asked if KPIs are the nemesis of innovation.

I am asking these questions of directors, boards, senior leadership teams and data/ data managers. Directors are accountable in law for removing discrimination and ensuring health and safety (S.172 Companies Act[104]), but how can we act on knowledge without understanding the structure or framing of this data? If we assume – that is a risk.

> Ask yourself and your business the following questions:

1. Do we have a data philosophy, and if so, what is it?

2. What is the structure of our data for each silo?
   Is there a single top-level ontology?

3. Do we know the structure/ ontologies of data throughout our ecosystem?

4. What is the attestation and rights of the data in Our Data Lake?
   How do we check if we are using data for a different purpose than intended?

5. How would we detect the consequences in our decision making by the aggregation of data with different ontologies?

For most, this is already too much detail and in the weeds!

If you want to go deeper into this topic, this is a fantastic paper: A survey of Top-Level Ontologies to inform the ontological choices for a Foundation Data Model[105].

Summary

In business, we want to use data to make better decisions and create more value. However, we must recognise that the data we use has a structure (ontology). Our data's very structure (designed or otherwise) creates bias, preventing certain outcomes from being created, and creating others. The reality is that our structures (ontologies) have already committed our data strategy and business model to success or failure.

The reality is that our structures (ontologies) have already committed our data strategy and business model to success or failure.

As a leader, have you questioned what the structure (ontology) of your data is? Has your team informed you of the limitations that your data structure/ontology places on decision making? To ensure that these limitations are properly considered, the Chief Data Officer (CDO[106]) should be tasked with providing a map, matrix or translation table, showing the linkage of datasets to ontologies, and the resulting implications.

As we now depend on business ecosystem data, do you know the ontologies of others in your ecosystem and how that affects your decision-making capability? Gaps in data sharing[107] ontologies affect decisions and create Quantum Risk[108]. Understanding what assumptions we make about data is essential for mitigating investment risk. Currently, we are using public ESG data to make capital allocation decisions without knowing where the data came from, what ontology the data has, or if the right analysis tools have been used.

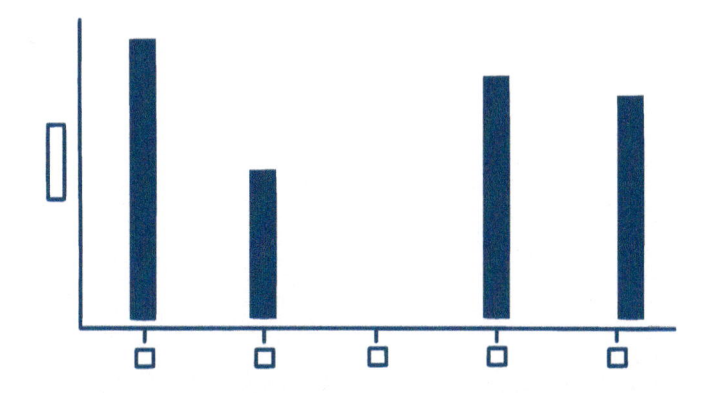

Implication 1: Management and leadership

The figure-of-8 diagram (figure 3, below) shows two interconnected loops. This connection is the mindset of the leader. Outstanding leadership, with an open mindset, can choose which loop is best at this time. Poor leadership will stick to the lower, closed mindset loop. The lower loop never starts with a different way of asking questions or solving problems. Those in this self-confirming loop stick to the same biases, decisions and paradigms. This creates the perception of a singular, fixed culture - "we have our way of doing it". The approach is consistent, the methods are highly efficient and based on the $1bn profit last year, we know it works, and we should continue to do the same. The reward mechanisms, KPIs and balanced scorecards are structured to keep the same highly efficient and effective thinking. This model of thinking assumes that yesterday, today and tomorrow will create the same outcomes, if we continue to do the same. There is nothing wrong with this, and during times of stability, many have made vast fortunes with this approach.

Great leaders follow this loop when it is suitable, but can also swap to the upper loop if needed. Such leaders sense an incoming change, a "paradigm shift[109]"; a concept identified by the American physicist and philosopher Thomas Kuhn. The paradigm shift is defined as *"a fundamental change in the basic concepts and experimental practices of a scientific discipline"*, and means there is a new structure to understand (ontology). The new structure brought in by the paradigm shift means that there is a need to determine the new culture, to create value within a new structure. Together, a team will form an approach. At this point, the team will question the shift and the assumptions that have led to change, setting a new mindset for the new order.

Critically - understanding structure and ontology is crucial, and it is why I believe Data Philosophy, Data Ontology and better decisions based on data are current board issues. Still, they require new skills, are highly detailed, and often require a mind shift.

Figure 3: Understanding structure and ontology is crucial for a data-driven digital board

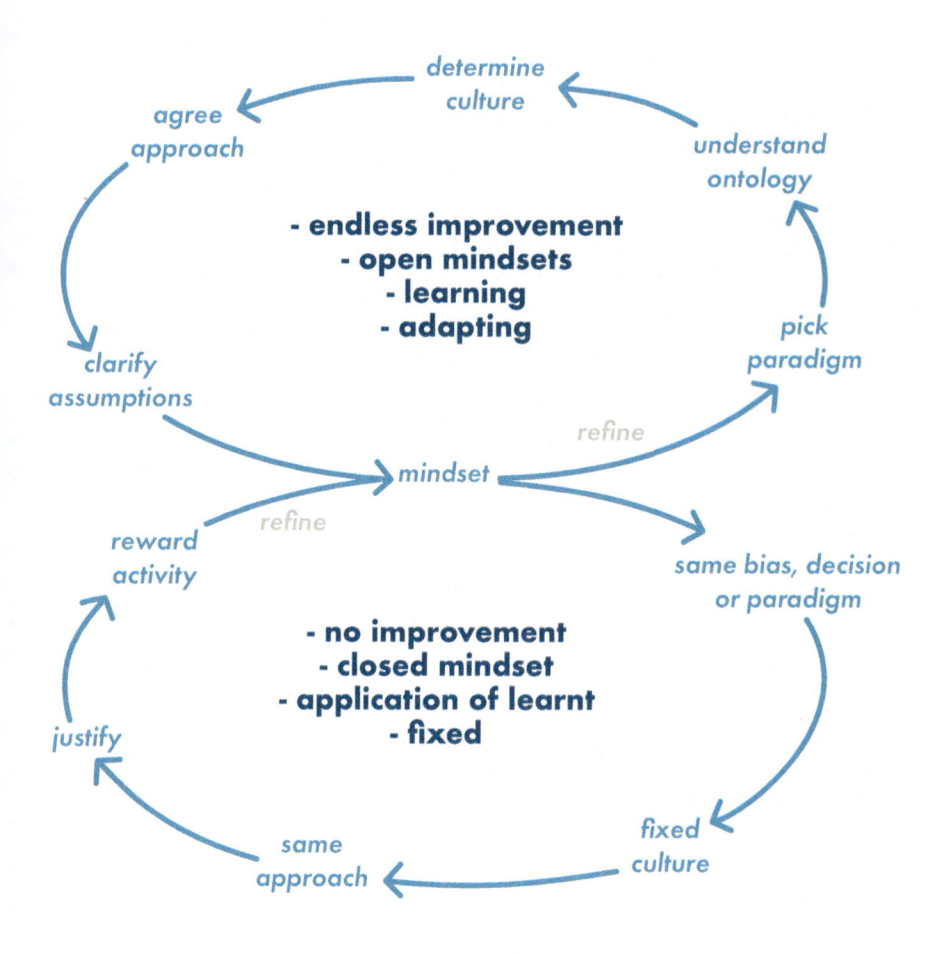

Implication 2: AI and automation

The Data Paradox: how are you supposed to know how to create questions about something that you did not know we had to question?

Every child reads a book differently. A child learns to use questions to check and refine understanding. Every software engineer reads code differently. A software engineer is forced to check their understanding of the code and function, by asking questions and by being asked questions. Whilst every AI will make sense of the data differently (ontology and code), right now, an AI cannot check its understanding of data by asking questions! Who could/ would/ should the AI ask the clarification question of, and how do we check the person who answered is without bias? (Note: I am not referring to active question-answering agents (AQA[110])).

Sherlock Holmes in The Great Game says *"people do not like telling you things; they love to contradict you. Therefore, if you want smart answers, do not ask a question. Instead, give a wrong answer or ask a question in such a way that it already contains the wrong information. It is highly likely that people will correct you"*. Do you do this to your data, or can you do this to your AI?

As of September 2023, we cannot write an "algorithm" that detects if AI is going to create harm (evil). This is partly because we cannot agree on the definition of "harm", so we cannot determine the unintended consequences, and we cannot bound harm for a person vs society.

There is a drive towards automation for efficiency based on the analysis of data. As a director, are you capable of asking the right questions to determine which biases and prejudices are created in the automated processes, the data structures, different ontologies, and data attestation, or to detect bias in the processes? This is crucial, given that directors are accountable and responsible - however, this is a skill that the whole board needs. Where is the audit and quota for these skills - can you prove that they are available to the board?

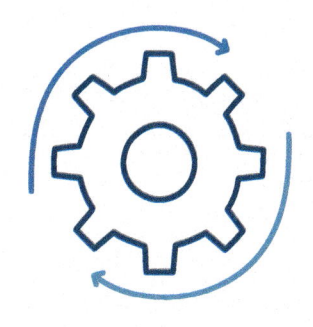

Chapter 8 - Part two

Data framing affects your perception of everything

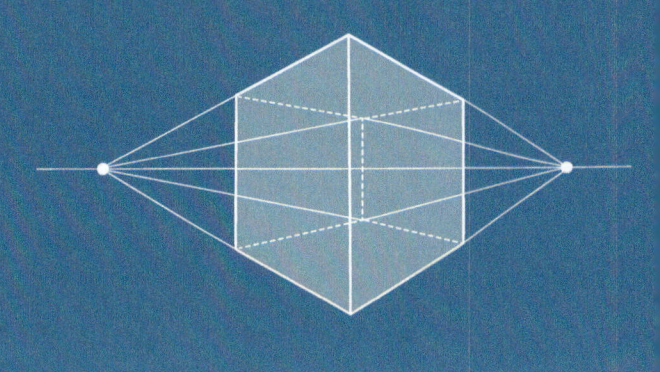

This section explores why data ontology is critical and the links to governance, oversight and better decisions. It presents a totally new way of organising your data, so you can talk about its value in leadership and board meetings

How to value data

Figure 1: A Theory of Sensemaking[111]*

DATA
recognise/ construct a frame

FRAME
manage attention and define, connect and filter the data

ELABORATION CYCLE

REFRAMING CYCLE

QUESTION A FRAME
- track anomalies
- detect inconsistencies
- judge plausability
- gauge data quality

ELABORATE A FRAME
- add and fill slots
- seek and infer data
- discover new data /new relationships
- discard data

REFRAME
- compare frames
- seek a new frame

PRESERVE

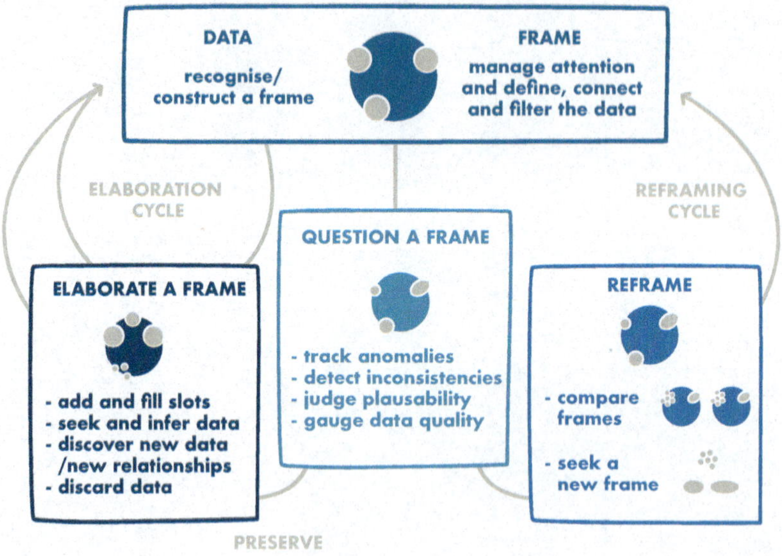

There are many unsaid or unspoken assumptions/ framings/ perceptions that we assume are true when we come together to discuss data. A few of these are listed here:

- The more data we have, the better decisions we can make

- We all know what data is

- Privacy rules apply to all data

- Better data means less risk

- All we need is better data policies, frameworks, regulation, policing and oversight

---

[111] https://www.researchgate.net/figure/The-Data-Frame-Theory-of-Sensemaking-The-Data-Frame-Theory-of-Sensemaking-consists-of_fig2_253238532

However, more data creates new risks and not necessarily better outcomes. This is because we lack a coherent structure to test assumptions, ask better questions and determine if our tools and data are aligned. More policies and rules only create more opportunities in the gaps between them. This section of chapter 8 presents a method for rethinking your data. Because it is new, and allows everyone to have a voice, it opens up space to discuss these unsaid assumptions.

We explored in the last chapter that the analogy of "data is oil" represents a complex idea in a simple linear narrative, which once questioned, soon falls apart.

Data is not oil, sunshine, labour or anything else, and the reality is that "Data is Data" - and we have not fully realised the value or harm of this technology. Describing data as a "technology" is similar to applying the definition to "life", the earth's oldest technology. Technology is the application to matter that achieves something reproducible. Data, and life, are not neutral, and the value and harm of both are complex. Just like aesthetics (beauty), data and life create division and inequality for individuals. What type of data you have, and the value of that data to you and others is a complicated question to unpack, principally because the value of data is context dependent and varies greatly based on numerous factors, such as:

- **Utility and relevance:** The value of data depends on how useful and relevant it is to a specific task or objective. Data that provides actionable insights or answers critical questions can be highly valuable to some, who also ignore small or apparently low-quality data because it appears to have less or no value. But anthropology (a discipline of study which focuses on small data) creates revolutionary potential.

- **Scarcity and availability:** Data that is rare or difficult to obtain can be more valuable, especially if it provides a competitive advantage. Conversely, data that is abundant and easily accessible might have a lower value. However, as machine learning and language models have revealed, scale matters for training data and recognising different biases.

- **Monetisation opportunities:** Data can be valuable when it can be used to create new margins or income. However, targeted advertising, personalised services, and data-driven products create new risks and fines, and cross-the-creepy-line, destroying brand value.

- **Accuracy and trustworthiness:** Accurate and trustworthy data is apparently more valuable since it leads to more reliable insights and decisions. However, determining what is inaccurate or unreliable data can lead to costs that outweigh any value that could be gained.

- **Privacy and ethical considerations:** The value of data can be influenced by concerns about privacy, security, and ethical considerations. Valuable data might lose its value if its collection or use violates privacy laws or ethical norms.

- **Economic impact:** The value of data can be measured by the economic impact it has. Data-driven insights can lead to cost savings, process improvements, and innovation, all contributing to economic value.

- **Potential insights:** The value of data lies in the insights and knowledge it can provide. Valuable data has the potential to reveal patterns, trends, and correlations that were previously unknown.

- **Long-term value:** Some data might have value that is not immediately apparent, but can become clear over time as new technologies, algorithms, or use cases emerge.

Thus far, for those who live in a data-driven world, this description offers nothing new. Still, it is worth stating that the variables bound an economic view of data, as do the specific contexts, goals, and potential benefits associated with its use. Organisations and industries will place different values on any dataset, based on their unique needs and objectives.

Data demands something new and different

I have realised, as I write this book, that my own framing of data has become increasingly foggy and messy. When I wrote "My Digital Footprint" back in 2008, I used a value chain structure of collect, store, analyse and action as the way to describe different value-adding activities for data. Since then, I have written many times that for data to have value in a commercial sense, we need [better attestation and confirmed rights](#)[112], as data is an artefact of the technology, business and economic systems we have. **I realise that these ideas, too, are restrictive and limiting.** Data has a layered richness, which we can explore through different lenses, including the complexity of extracting value, the messiness of combining it or how it is created. Data is, of itself, not an economy - that comes from the use and application of data.

It appears that a good first question may be [**"What is the purpose of our data?"**](#)[113], as set out in Chapter 7. However, understanding why it is valuable is more complicated than we think, as we need a structure, framework and [data ontology](#)[114] to be able to unpick the why. This was the focus of the previous section, in which I said that "structures are ontologies, which are philosophies." This concept needs a little more unpacking, before we can learn something new.

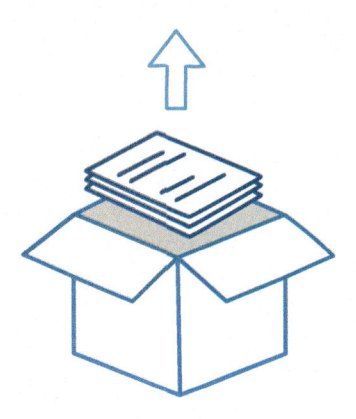

Figure 2: How standards proliferate[115*]

Situation: There are 14 competing standards.

14?! Ridiculous! We need to develop one universal standard that covers everyone's use cases. Yeah!

Soon: Situation: There are 15 competing standards.

Ontology[116] is a branch of metaphysics[117] (philosophy) which deals with the nature of being. It provides a set of concepts and categories in a specific subject area or domain, and shows their properties and the relations between each one. Ontology matters because it can now be created automatically from large datasets. Top-Level ontologies[118] are notoriously difficult, and there is always one example or case that does not fit. So, just like standards, a new top-level is needed. Below, the new framing is not a top-level ontology, this is an **ontology to frame the dataset(s) we have inside an organisation and its ecosystem.**

Here are four categories that data can be categorised into. However, before we expand on the categories - **Never Been Alive, Dead, Living** and **Alive** data - remember that each of these has value. **I believe they all have equal value, based on the opening commentary of ascribing value.**

These categories do not form a pyramid of data that we desire to scramble to the top of, nor are they a foundation to build on, where true value rests somewhere else. There is no best category to be in; these are simply statements to describe our data by characteristics. This ontology is built on the view that there is equal value in the data represented in each category. Therefore, they help us recognise the differences in data categories - which is important because this holds the insights for directors, boards and decision making. Absolutely, there are grey areas and data in the gaps, but that is the joy of data and life - there is only complexity in its structure. After expanding on the descriptions, we will unpack the tools and governance of these different data categories, **as this is what enables leadership to excel.**

---

[115] https://imgs.xkcd.com/comics/standards.png

The categories are outlined below. In each case, I will be unpacking a new perspective and using analogies from nature as the basis of the category.

1 - Data that has never been alive

Data that has never been alive - The framing for data included in this category is to consider everything about us that has never been alive. For example, water, rocks, minerals, elements, gold and right now, lithium - these all have massive economic value. This category would include ideas that have been crafted for a purpose, such as cement, bronze, steel, buildings and property. Elements have been combined to make better materials. Data from weather, space, buildings and supply chains are good examples of never-been-alive data. Value is independent of the activities, but this data enables control and tells stories. A significant proportion of data in your ecosystem and organisation falls into this category.

2 - Dead data

Dead data - Death is the irreversible cessation of all biological functions that sustain an organism. Dead data is data that cannot sustain an organisation. Dead data looks like coal, oil, gas and wood. Something was alive (tree), but in death, a different value proposition has been created. There is massive economic value in dead stuff. Dead data includes lifeless data. If you describe objects or machines as lifeless, you mean that they are not living things, even though they may resemble living things. Fire can appear to be alive, because it moves. Dead things have stored energy but have lost attestation and providence. A massive amount of data in a digital business has been collected from something that was living, but because identity has been removed, analysis is undertaken, and compression has happened, this data does not represent the living. But that does reduce its value. Data may appear to represent your business, but in reality, it does not. All training data for ML and LLM (Large Language Models) is dead data, along with all meta-data.

3 - Living data

Living data – having life; being alive; not dead, in actual existence or use. Living systems self-assemble and heal. They can replicate, survive, flourish and adapt to almost all environments. Plants and animals are living, but they are not aware of themselves or the consequences of their existence. Oranges are unaware they are orange. Whilst [Wisdom and Knowledge are just more data][119], the knowledge, insights, information and wisdom created by systems provide living data. This can help in automation, but the data is unaware of itself. All the data that you use for automation is in this category, as well as anything you use to interrogate the health and status of the overall system. Reporting, oversight and compliance data, along with data for identity, attestation and providence, all rest here. I agree with the criticism that this data cannot self-assemble and heal, yet…

4 - Alive data

Alive data – Having life, and being in a state where an organism can perform independent functions beyond survival. And, for the most part, is able to contribute to survival - this, in general, is a definition of being alive. The organism has an awareness, which is something that humans and many animals have. The future (near) holds the possibility that AI systems will also gain awareness of both the self and other - however, the ability to act and have agency are aspects to be debated. Being alive, aware and having agency enables independent decision making, conversation, and the ability to grow as an entity and create things that don't physically exist (time, money, economics, companies). Where is such data, and does it have value? It is data we create about us, for us. Behavioural economics and personalisation depend on this dataset. It is us, it is our action and labour, and the value we can create is growing rapidly.

Next, it is worth considering these four concepts before we get to the implications of decision making and governance.

- **Data sharing:** Obviously, sharing data within a category is not a problem, however, sharing data across categories creates new data, and deciding in which category the new data sits is not an easy or obvious question to answer.

- **The half-life of data:** In this case, the half-life of data refers to the amount of time it takes for the majority of it to become irrelevant. This is supposedly a downward exponential curve, meaning that data is at its peak value when first collected, then accelerates in loss of value over time. Within this new framing, the half-life idea is not true. But it highlights that framing has encouraged us to be obsessed with new real-time data and to move on from the data we already have - and its existing value.

- **Tools and practices:** The tools we need for collecting, storing and analysing data in each of the categories, Never Been Alive, Dead, Living and Alive, are different. Further, the practices, methods, rules and systems we need for each category depend on the silo. Yes, there are a few tools and analytical methods that are equally applicable to a number of categories, but that does not mean they are the right ones, or are being applied in the right way.

- **Risk; small and big data:** Whilst the nature of risk changes with data size, it is probable that the actual impact or harm does not. Decisions taken from small data have risk, and equally, decisions from large data have risk, and they are different. Anthropology should be as equally valued as statistics, as both shed light uniquely on how to manage uncertainty.

Decision making and governance

The purpose of thinking about data using the Never Been Alive, Dead, Living, and Alive categories is that it allows us to answer "what do we need data for, today?" and further, "what do we need data for, tomorrow?" We can then discuss whether the data we have can be optimised for the outcome we want, or not. This is about choices, decision making and judgement, and asking if we have, or are we applying, the right tools to the data we have or need, that will enable better decisions.

It is obvious that most business and management tools are designed to encourage repetition of what we have done before, with the sole purpose of becoming ever more efficient and effective at it. This framing of siloed optimising and the processes we have installed, along with our incentives and culture, are all designed to prevent us from unpacking the realities of data for our organisation.

If we want to do and deliver something different, we must realise that there is a dependence on governance as the process that allows us to balance many aspects that are limited by resources, bound by perception and framed by choice. For me, governance is a wicked problem – insomuch that it cannot be fixed, there is no single solution to the problem, and "wicked" as it denotes resistance from parties to finding a resolution.

Here is the rub: the wickedness of governance is that it has to be holistic, and must embrace and equally value both mechanistic (complicated) and organic (complex) skills and abilities.

- If you leave a book on a table for a year, it will still be on the table, and you need to know that it is mechanistic and repeatable.

- If you leave some fresh fruit on the same table for a year, it will not be there. Whilst this is good to know, it does not help where or if there will be a table – uncertainty.

For better decisions, we need governance, and governance depends on these two fundamentals/ foundations: one, of repeatability and stability (demanding resilience and coping with ambiguity and volatility). The other enables us to sit with uncertainty and complexity. One is bonded to what has happened before, and one provides the bridge to what can happen next (there are risks in both, and they, as well as harm and impact, are different).

A well-published fact in social science is that a society needs to equally value both bonded and bridged[120] individuals and mindsets to be successful and thrive. Equally, governance demands that we must balance its two personalities: bonded (to what we are doing) and bridged (to what we can/ will do).

- **Bonded governance –** Delivers resilience, is rational, reliant on best practice, is driven by standards, is highly repetitive, formulaic, instructive, process-driven, and depends on data. Bonded governance addresses all the known: known, known: unknown and unknown: known risks. Experience of asking the right question is critical. As a framework, it can be taught and examined. The bulk of board meetings, compliance, and oversight heavy lifting is here, and we continually try to codify and simplify it, as bonded governance yields an accurate perception of what is currently going on with associated risk. Bonded governance stops before it considers the unintended consequences of our decisions, which is explored in bridged governance. We are good at bonded governance as it is delivered by the training, coaching, mentoring and education systems we have today.

But we can always improve.

- **Bridged governance –** Is curious, adaptive, responsive, instinctive, open, and depends on small signals in lots of noise. Bridged governance enables individuals to address all the unknown: unknowns. Mindset is critical and should be driven by better questions. Bridged governance demands our time and ability to live with ambiguity, complexity and uncertainty, as its output is an improved sense of direction and navigation. We are hopeless at bridged governance as it takes time, is complex to teach and nearly impossible to examine and test. This is where difficulty persists, and many avoid this by calling bridged governance soft, or framing it as a diversion. Philosophy (Aesthetics, Epistemology, Ethics, Logic, Metaphysics) becomes a critical aspect in decision making as there are no facts, truths or attestation. It is where judgement is learned and sense-making honed, as these skills improve our ability to find better choices for bonded governance.

Each director must have both personalities/ perspectives/ skills. It is not necessary for teams to create balance; this is about individuals being able to operate in both domains (often simultaneously). Both demand data, but different data. Both need tools and skills, but they are contextual and situational.

This is why siloed thinking about data is so dangerous for a board. Implementing best practices is a solid and valid idea, but such ideals can only be applied to the bonded aspect of governance and, further, only when there is certainty and ubiquity. Structures, processes, methodology and checklists do not work in times of uncertainty as a way to discharge your legal duties as a director.

A few reflective questions

1. Which ontology do you use for data across your company and ecosystem?

2. How do you check if you are applying the right tools, processes and methods for the dataset you have?

3. Have any executive decisions been made recently, where there is a potential mismatch between the tools and the data structure?

4. Can your governance deliver an accurate perception of what is going on, right now?

5. Does your governance provide a sense of direction and navigation?

6. How do we know we can trust our data, tools, and governance? Are they good enough to discharge our fiduciary duties?

Chapter 8 - Part three

Is the data presented to you enabling a real choice?

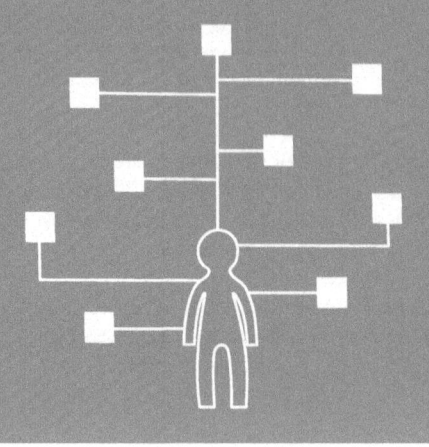

This chapter unpacks why senior leaders need to develop skills to see past big, noticeable, loud noises (data) and uncover small signals, if we want to enable a board that makes the necessary challenging judgement calls.

During his opening keynote at Innotribe/ SIBOS 2019[121], Prof Brian Cox said the following, give or take: "if you cannot find it in nature, it is not natural". This got me thinking about how choice is created, and how we then make decisions and judgements. How humans choose, decide and make complex judgements draws heavily on psychology and the behavioural sciences. Alongside judgement, I have a polymath interest in quantum mechanics, the microbiome and consciousness. I was relaxing and watching "His Dark Materials[122]", which it turns out was worth hanging in for, and had finished Stuart Russell's[123] "Human Compatible", and Carlo Rovelli's[124] "The Order of Time". Finally, whilst watching this BBC mini-series[125] about free will, this chapter emerged. "Choice" assumes that you have agency, and can choose or make a decision. But how is choice possible when the foundations that we are built on/ from do not have a choice? Can data give us a choice?

Signals, signals and damn noise

Decision: the action or process of deciding something, or of resolving a question. A decision is an act of or need for making up one's mind.

Choice: an act of choosing between two or more possibilities. It requires a right, agency, or opportunity to choose.

The etymology of the two words add important context. The word decision comes from "cutting off", whilst choice comes from "to perceive." Therefore, a decision is more about process orientation, meaning we are going through analysis and steps to eliminate or cut off options. With choice, it is more of an approach, meaning there is a perception of what the outcome of a particular choice may be. Because of this, let's now run with choice rather than decision.

A decision is about going through analysis and steps to eliminate or cut off options. Choice is an approach, meaning there is a perception of what the outcome may be.

Does energy have a choice?

Figure 1: We are using energy as respresented by a magnetic field

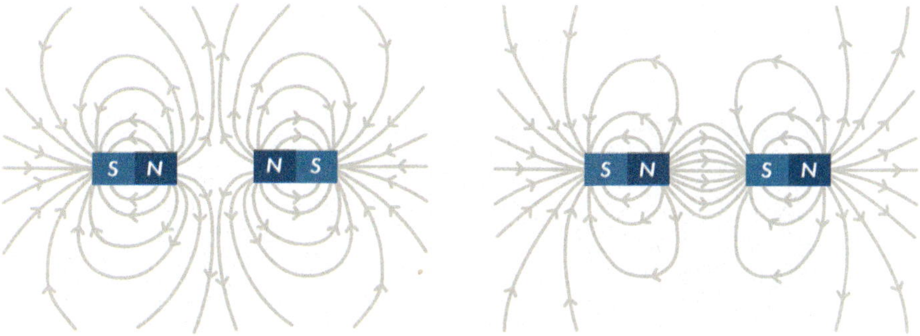

(A)

(B)

Two magnets, north and south. Irrespective of position, they must attract one another. Do they have a choice?

Three magnets, north, north, south. They have a more complicated relationship - position and distance now matter and will influence the actual outcome. But there is no choice; the rules define the outcome.

At the majority of starting positions for the three magnets, there is only one outcome, and as such, choice is predetermined. However, there are several possible situations in which many magnets are sufficiently far apart, and there are only small forces at play (far-field).

In this case, the movement between possible outcomes may appear to be more random. Any specific outcome is based on a small and unseen momentary influence. The more magnets that are exerting small forces, the more random a positional change or choice may appear, as the level of complexity of the model increases beyond what is rational.

Therefore, at a simple model of three magnets, there is no choice. Whereas, in a complicated model with many magnets, it would appear that a degree of randomness or chaos is introduced (entropy). The simple model does not exist in nature as it is impossible to remove small signals, even if they are hidden because of large-close forces.

At this level of abstraction, energy itself does not have a choice. The outcome is predictable, as there are indeed a fixed number of possible outcomes, which can be modelled.

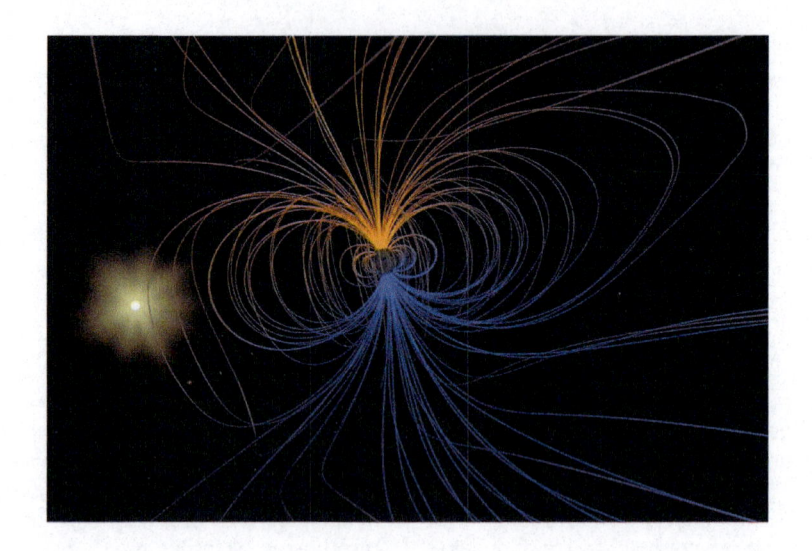

Figure 2: Energy[126*]

Stick with me here – we are exploring something that we don't often want to face up to as leaders. How would you feel if you realised that, as a board, we do not make the decisions that we can be truly accountable and responsible for, as in reality there is no choice?

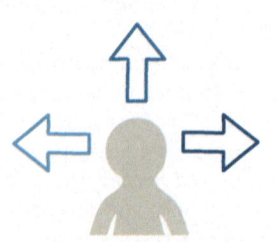

[126*] https://svs.gsfc.nasa.gov/vis/a000000/a003800/a003822/magnetic_field_cover.png

There are only three fundamental forces of energy, each governed by their own rules

1 - Gravity

There is only one kind of charge: mass/energy, which is always attractive. There's no upper limit to how much mass/energy you can have, as the worst you can do is create a black hole, which still fits into our theory of gravity. Every quantum of energy, whether it has a rest mass (like an electron) or not (like a photon), curves the fabric of space, causing the phenomenon that we perceive as gravitation.

If gravitation turns out to be quantum in nature, there's only one quantum particle, the graviton, required to carry the gravitational force. Based on established maths and models, gravity suggests there is no choice, as the graviton is always attractive. As we know from our study of things such as our galaxy the Milky Way, a single force introduces many patterns and an appearance of randomness. However, with enough observations and data, it can be modelled - it is predictable.

2 - Electromagnetism

A fundamental force that readily appears on macroscopic scales, and gives us a little more basic variety. Instead of one type of electric charge, there are two: positive and negative. Like charges repel; opposite charges attract. Although the detail of the physics underlying electromagnetism is very different from the physics underlying gravitation, its structure is still straightforward in the same way that gravitation is.

You can have free charges, of any magnitude, with no restrictions, and there's only one particle required (the photon) to mediate all the possible electromagnetic interactions. Based on the established maths and models, there is no choice here. However, as we know from our study of, say, light waves, we will get many patterns and an appearance of randomness.

3 - The strong nuclear force

The strong nuclear force is one of the most puzzling features of the universe. Here, the rules become fundamentally different. Instead of one type of charge (gravitation) or even two (electromagnetism), there are three fundamental charges for the strong nuclear force. Inside every proton or neutron-like particle, there are at least three quark[127] and antiquark combinations - but just how many is unknown, as the list keeps growing.

Gluons[128] are the particles that mediate the strong force, and after this, it gets messy. It is worth noting that we don't have the maths or an established model to frame this, but it appears that there is still ultimately no choice as we cannot have a net charge of any type (how it balances is well beyond me). However, as we know from studies using the Large Hadron Collider[129] at CERN, the strong nuclear force is quantum[130] in nature and has a property that means it only exists when observed.

In nature, we have one, two or many forces, and each can create structure and randomness. But can anything in nature truly make a choice or decision?

Following this, does information have a choice?

Two magnets, north and south, but information now defines distance and strength. Therefore, information determines that there can only be one outcome. The observer knowing the information can only ever observe the single outcome — three magnets facing off, north, north, south. A complicated relationship, but position, distance and field strength are known; therefore, the outcome can be modelled and predicted.

Further, we can now move to a dynamic model, in which each of the magnets rotates and moves during the measured period. What happens when the available information includes the future probability position of the magnets? Does information enable the magnets not to move right away, as they know that it will not change the outcome and they could instead conserve energy? (This being a fundamental law of thermodynamics).

As with unpacking the onion, this metaphor is overly simplistic, as gravity and electromagnetism are defined and bound by the Laws of Relativity and Thermodynamics. In contrast, the strong nuclear force is defined and bound by the Laws of Quantum. Gravity and electromagnetism are deterministic in nature as there is no choice of direction, as per the laws. The interaction of a complex system can make something look random, but when removed from time and point observation, these laws define the patterns that we see.

However, the strong nuclear force being quantum means we don't know its state until we observe it; which fully supports the idea of chaos/ randomness, and perhaps something closer to being presented with a choice (aka free will). It is not so much "you can do anything", more that you can pick between states; rather than just following a defined or a predetermined flow to this point, bound by the foundational laws of relativity. Does information have a quantum property, insomuch that it is only when the observer looks and can act, that it becomes that state? Think carefully about this, in the context of bias.

Can information or knowledge enable choice?

Does information require energy, and if so, does the very nature of an informational requirement change outcomes? (Heisenberg Uncertainty Principle[131]). Can something determine that to minimise energy expenditure it should wait, in case a lower energy requirement with a better outcome comes by later? How would the information know whether to make that decision or choice? What rule would it be following?

In such a situation, we are asking that, based on information, the general rules of choice and decision making are ignored. In this instance, we would step over the first outcome or requirement, preferring to take a later option. Has information now built an experience, which feeds into knowledge? What even is information in this context? Consider the colour of petals or leaves in autumn. Science reveals that colour is a derivative of visible light. A red leaf reflects wavelengths longer than those that a green leaf reflects. Colour is a property not of the leaf, but of how the leaf interacts with light, the eye, and our ability to describe it with common sound (words). This analogy assumes the observer has the right level of vitamin C and a healthy brain structure, which would otherwise add further considerations. In summary, what we think of as intrinsic properties (information) of the world are merely the effects of multiple causes coinciding, or many small signals. In this sense, reality is not so much made up of physical things, but interactions and flow. The same applies to touch and smell.

Intrinsic properties (information) are merely the effects of multiple causes coinciding.

Remember - we are considering how we get to make a choice, based on the idea that if it does not appear in nature, it is probably not natural. Have we convinced ourselves that complexity creates free will?

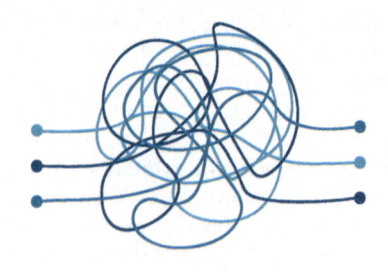

Free will, can you make a decision?

Now we can reflect on the title question - **is the data presented to you enabling a real choice?** Given that choice and free will require that you have agency and can choose or decide, we now reach a second question: how can free will be possible when the foundations of information (energy types) you are building on do not appear to create choice? Yes, the appearance of randomness; yes, which only exists on observation - but does that create choice?

We have to admire those tiny signals which present themselves as choices at scale, as nothing has an overall significant effect. Everything has a flow. Does this lack of a dominant signal create the illusion of free will, or ability to make a choice? When the signals are big, loud and noisy, drawing out small signals, is choice taken away?

Executive leadership

Looking at what makes great leadership, it is not simply that we are programmed in this way. Rather, it is that great leaders are highly tuned and responsive to small signals that most of us don't know are there because we are too busy, or focussed on following instructions.

Great leadership demands the ability to access small signals to be able to exercise judgement. However, is our love of traffic light dashboards, summaries, 1-minute overviews, elevator pitches, priorities, urgency, fast meetings, executive summaries and KPIs creating data-driven management signals which can only focus on the "priority" loud, noisy signals? The more layers and filters that data passes through, the more smaller signals are lost. Instead, we are left with an increasing loudness pointing us towards one path, with no ability to make a true decision and a removal of choice. Does the increasing domination of loud signals mean we reduce our leadership's sensitivity, to only see the obvious? We then blame this same leadership for not sensing the market signals, not being responsive, nor following the lead that others do!

Decisions (choice) or judgement

Human brains are constructed or wired to create and discover patterns, to which we ascribe meaning and learning. Signals help us form and be informed about the shaping of and changes within patterns, and their alignment to other patterns. Therefore, we love signals that help us form or manage patterns, which we call rules and heuristics.

Management theory teaches and rewards us for prioritising signals, especially the loud, noisy, obvious ones that are easy to see and understand. A useful example is of a cloud (one in the sky, not a server farm) - it is an unmistakable signal. A cloud is right here, right now. It is big and obvious.

Clouds are a data point; observing clouds provides us with highly structured single-source data. The data we collect about the clouds in front of us is given to our data science team, who will present back their insights on the data that is collected, giving us all sorts of new information and knowledge about that data. Big signals win. The statistics team takes the same dataset, and provides forecasts and probabilities based on maths, inferring insights based on data that is not there. The outcome from both teams may be different, but they both present us with significant overriding signals telling us what decision to make, based on the cloud's data.

Figure 3: Deriving data from signals

clouds are markers or signals; you are observing the system

clouds are data points; you are observing the boundary

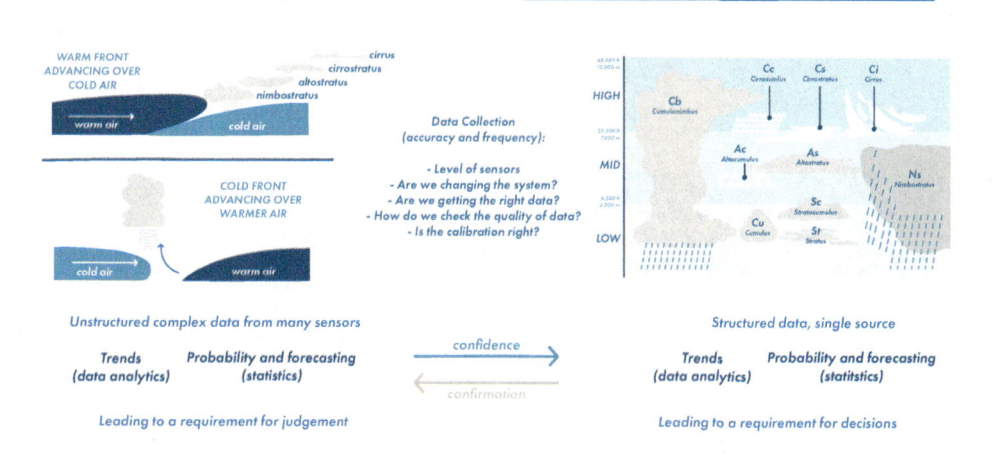

Unstructured complex data from many sensors

Data Collection (accuracy and frequency):
- Level of sensors
- Are we changing the system?
- Are we getting the right data?
- How do we check the quality of data?
- Is the calibration right?

Structured data, single source

Trends (data analytics) | Probability and forecasting (statistics)

confidence →
← confirmation

Trends (data analytics) | Probability and forecasting (statitstics)

Leading to a requirement for judgement

Leading to a requirement for decisions

171

Another approach is to look at the system: how and why did the cloud form? Where did it appear? Where is it going? By gathering lots of data from different sources and seeking many signals, we can look at systems. Sensors are detecting light level, wind direction and speed, ground temperature, air temperature for 100 kilometres around and 25 high - lots of delicate low signal data. However, it is unstructured data. Once we have fed the data into the teams, the data analytics team brings knowledge of the system, its complexity, and what we know based on the data. The statistics team can provide forecasting and probability about clouds forming. Small signals, that collectively create choice and allow for judgement. Our small signals give confidence that our models work, as we have cloud data and that cloud data confirms that our signals are picking up our environmental cues.

Side note: the differences in "data analysis" using data science or statistics. Whilst both data scientists and statisticians use data to make inferences about a data subject, they will approach the issue of data analysis quite differently. For a data scientist, data analysis is sifting through vast amounts of data: inspecting, cleaning, modelling, and presenting in a non-technical way to non-data scientists. The vast majority of this data analysis is performed on a computer. A data analyst will have a data science toolbox (e.g. programming languages like Python and R, or experience with frameworks like Hadoop and Apache Spark) with which they can investigate the data and make inferences.

A statistician, however, instead of vast amounts of data, will have a limited amount of information in the form of a sample (i.e. a portion of the population) and data analysis will be performed on this sample, using rigorous statistical techniques. A statistical analyst will generally use mathematical-based techniques like hypothesis testing[132], probability[133], and various statistical theorems to make inferences. Although much of a statistician's data analysis can be performed with the help of statistical programs such as R, the analysis is more methodical and targeted to understanding one particular aspect of the sample at a time (for example, the mean[134], standard deviation[135] or confidence interval[136]).

These data analysis approaches are fundamentally different and produce different signals; for a full story, we often need both.

Does a leadership team choose or decide?

As a senior leader, executive or director, you have to face the reality of this chapter right now. Currently, you have four significant noisy signals to contend with. That is, critical parts of your company are presenting you with large signals, using:

- Statistical analysis based on an observable point
- Data science analysis based on an observable point
- Statistical analysis based on a system
- Data science analysis based on a system

Do you know which type of significant loud signals you are being given, and if they are drowning out all the small signals that you should be sensing? Who sits around the decision-making table, and are they sensing the small signals? Are you being presented with a decision, or are you being guided to a favourable outcome based on someone else's reward or motivation? How do you understand the bias present in the data and analysis, and find the small signals? Indeed, to quote @scottdavid[137] *"You have to hunt for the paradoxes in the information being presented, because if you cannot see a paradox you are being framed into a one-dimensional model".*

Further, we need to grasp that data is also emerging outside of our control, from the wider ecosystem. This wider data has different ontologies, taxonomies and pedagogies - meaning that we will probably only discover signals and patterns within it that align with our framing, and that we miss external signals because they have a different structure.

Decision-making skills based on sensitivity

In September 2020, I wrote the article Leadership for "organisational fitness" is different from the leadership required for "organisational wellness"[138]. In the article, I explored the skills needed by executive leadership in decision making, to help a company be fit and well (which are different things).

The chart below highlights how, over a period of time, skills should be formed to enable individuals to work together with other professionals, who can deal with highly complex decision making (judgement). The axes are level of ability and expertise on the horizontal axis (x) and the decision environment on the vertical (y). The (0,0) point, where the axes cross, represents the moment at which we first learn to make decisions. Note that this has nothing to do with age or time. Starting from the lighter blue zone - this is where we make simple decisions. A bit like gravity, there is only one force at play, and one outcome. We are encouraged to find it and make the right choice (even though ultimately there is no choice.) The light grey areas on either side are where the "Peters Principle"[139] can be seen in practice; individuals act outside of their capacity and/ or are not given sufficient responsibility, and become disruptive. The white area is where most adults get to and stay. We understand, like electromagnetic forces, that there are two options or more.

We search out the significant signals, and those that bring us the reward to which we are aligned. We develop and hone our skills at making binary choices. The dark blue zone is where many senior executives get trapped, as they are unable to adapt - from acting in their own interests, to acting in the best interests of the organisation and ecosystem. This is because all their training focuses on how to perform better to serve their own interests and rewards (KPIs linked to bonuses). To move beyond the dark blue zone, we must create and build a whole new mental model. Like John Mayard Keynes[140], as we learn more, we make U-turns, adapt our thinking, change our philosophy, and adapt our behaviour. The lesson here is to never stop learning. At this point, we wrestle with quantum decision making, find we are looking for the small signals in the chaos, and need trusted advisors and equal peers. We seek out and find a paradox, never believing the data, the analysis, nor the steer that someone else is presenting. This is hard work but leads to better judgement, better decisions and better outcomes.

Figure 4: What skill, ability and expertise looks like in different decision environments

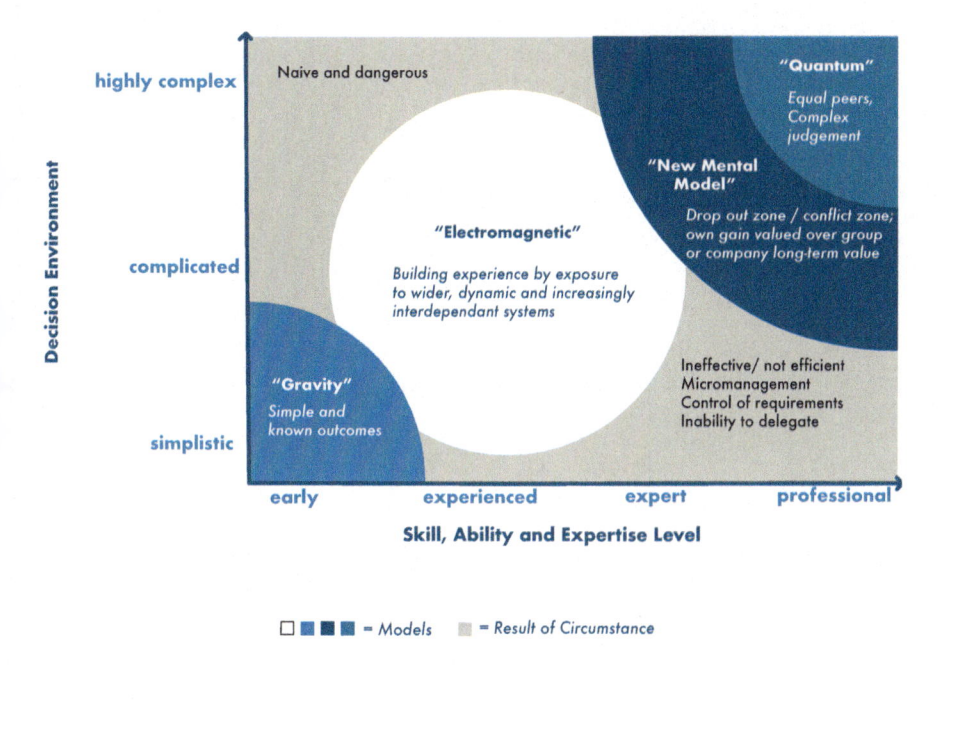

Decision Environment (y-axis): highly complex, complicated, simplistic
Skill, Ability and Expertise Level (x-axis): early, experienced, expert, professional

- Naive and dangerous
- "Quantum" — Equal peers, Complex judgement
- "New Mental Model" — Drop out zone / conflict zone; own gain valued over group or company long-term value
- "Electromagnetic" — Building experience by exposure to wider, dynamic and increasingly interdependant systems
- "Gravity" — Simple and known outcomes
- Ineffective/ not efficient, Micromanagement, Control of requirements, Inability to delegate

☐ ■ ■ ■ = Models   ■ = Result of Circumstance

Take away

Decisions are often not decisions; the choice is not always real, especially when the foundations of the choice are simple and binary. Leaders need to become very sensitive to signals, and find the weak and hidden ones to ensure that as complexity becomes a critical component of judgement, they are not forced to ratify choices. Ratification occurs when choices are not understood, the views are biassed, and the decision likely fulfils someone else's objectives.

As directors, we are held accountable and responsible for our decisions; we must take them to the best of our ability. As automation based on data becomes more prevalent in our companies, we have to become more diligent than ever if we are making judgements, choices or decisions. And, even if we are just ratifying something that has taken our choice away to fulfil its own bias and own dependency, using big signals.

Chapter 9

Quantum Risk: a wicked problem that emerges at the boundaries of our data dependency

I remain curious about how we can make better or wiser decisions. I am sharing this chapter as part of my own journey, as I unpack the mental boundaries and models that prevent me from making better decisions.

Who is king in the land of the blind risk monster?

In this chapter, I am fighting bias and prejudice regarding risk perceptions; please read the next few lines before you decide to stop. We tend to be blind to "risk" because we have all lived it, read about it, and listened to risk statements. Whether on the TV and radio for financial products, at the beginning of investment statements, for health and safety for machinery, for medicine, on the packets of cigarettes, or when you open that new app on your new mobile device. We are bombarded with endless risk statements that we assume we know the details of, or that we just ignore. There are more books on risk than on all other management and economics topics together. An entire field on the ontologies of risk exists; such is the significance of this topic. This chapter suggests that the entire established body of knowledge and expertise has missed something. A bold statement, but **quantum risk** is new, big, ugly, and already here - it's just that we are willingly blind to it.

At the end of the board pack or PowerPoint deck making the case for new investment, intervention, or for the adoption of the new model, there is a risk and assumptions list. We have seen these so many times that we don't actually read them. These statements are often copied, and the instances of risk statements inaccurately copied is significant; no effort is put in as such statements have become a habit in the process methodology. **The problem we all have with risk is that we think we know it all.** Quite frankly, we see risk as the prime reason to stop something, and occasionally manage it more closely, but never to understand something better. If you are operating a digital or data business, you face new risks that are not currently in your risk statement. You have not focussed on them before, you are unlikely to have been exposed to them, and this chapter will bring them to your attention. Is this worth 8 minutes of reading?

Many thanks to Peadar Duffy[141] whom I have been collaborating with on this thinking - he has published a super article on the same topic (quantum risk) here[142].

The purpose of business

We know that currently, 3% of Our Data Lake is financial data. Shockingly, 90% of our decisions are based on this sliver of data (Source: Google). We must aim for a better ratio of "data: decisions", and that includes non-financial data; by doing so, we will begin to make better decisions that have benefits beyond the shareholder primacy view of the world. As leaders, we have a desire to make the best possible decisions that we can. We fuse data, experience and knowledge to balance our perception of risk, probability and desired outcomes.

As mentioned in chapter 5, the well-publicised Business Roundtable August 2019 report[143] redefines a corporation's purpose as promoting "An economy that serves all… [Americans]". The idea that company purpose should align more closely with ecosystem thinking has been gaining prevalence since the 2008 financial crisis. This thinking has significant supporters, including Larry Fink[144], Blackrock's founder and CEO, who is an influential voice for ESG reporting and promotes the idea of changing decision-making criteria to achieve better outcomes. His yearly letters present an insightful journey.

Sir Donald Brydon's December 2019 report[145] highlights that governance and audit need attention if we are to deliver better decisions, with more transparency and accountability. The report concludes that audit has significant failings and our approach to tick box compliance is not serving directors, shareholders or society to the level expected. Given that so much of our risk management depends on the quality of the audit, internal and external, it is likely that we are overly confident in our unreliable data. The audit failure point alone could be sufficient exploration for this chapter; however, we are here to explore **Quantum Risk**. Quantum Risk only exists because of the business dependency we now have on data, which comes from our co-dependent supply chains and dependent ecosystems.

Quantum Risk is NEW

As a term from physics that describes the properties of particles, "quantum" will help us to understand new risk characteristics. The primary characteristics of quantum particle behaviour are the uncertainty principle, composite systems and entanglement. In business language, I understand these characteristics for Quantum risk as:

- **Uncertainty.** When you observe the same risk twice, it might not always be there, or it may look different.

- **Composite systems.** The same risk can be in many places simultaneously, but it is still only one risk.

- **Entanglement.** Your risk and my risk directly affect each other across our data ecosystem; they are coupled but may not be directly connected.

Framing Risk

Risk, like beauty, privacy, trust, transparency and many other ideals, is a personal perspective on the world. However, we all accept that we have to live with risk.

Understanding and managing risk fundamentally assumes that you can first *identify it*. If you cannot identify the risk, there appears to be nothing to consider or manage.

Having identified the risk, you can categorise and prioritise it using the classic impact vs likelihood model.

Figure 1: Risk management process

Identify Risk	Assess Risk
Control Risk	Review Controls

Figure 2: How the impact and likelihood of risk affects management

IMPACT

LIKELIHOOD	significant	moderate	minor
high	Extensive management essential	High management required	Manage and monitor risk
medium	Must manage to monitor risk	Management worthwhile	Accept and monitor risk
low	Considerable management required	May accept but monitor	Accept risk

Finally, the management (review and control) of risk determines if you are doing the right things to manage it, or if action is needed.

It is possible to add a third axis to a classic likelihood/ impact risk model, which is "quality of knowledge." This third axis visually highlights that a focus on high-risk scenarios accumulates the most knowledge. This is because "high risk" is where the management focus and control are required, which requires data, which becomes knowledge. If there is a **deficit** in knowledge because of poor data at any point in the matrix, the likelihood of hidden risk existing is increased. Poor data[146] (knowledge) can mean that either the impact (consequence) will be more severe or the likelihood (probability) is increased. In part, we can overcome the problems caused by poor data by recognising that such data always exists, but poor data easily hides the rather current issues of pandemics and systemic risk. However, if the *quality* of knowledge is based on erroneous data (data without rights and attestation[147]), we have no true understanding of the likelihood and impact of risk.

Figure 3: Available knowledge also affects management of risk

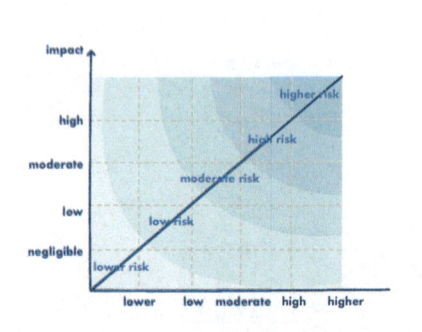

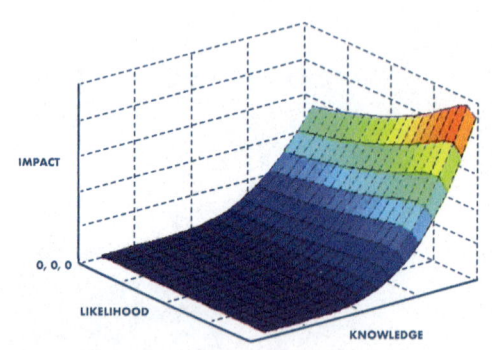

Some sophisticated models and maths have been created to help us qualify and understand the nature of risk, depending on its size and qualities. However, the list of risks that any one company faces is considered, defined and specified over a long period. Uncovering new risk is considered unlikely; however, as we are exploring here, it is more likely than we think. Given our natural confirmational bias towards risk (we know it), new risk is hard to identify.

Classic risk management models are created to help us gain certainty - where risk management is the identification, understanding, management and control of uncertainty.

Existing risk models are highly efficient within this frame of reference, and we can optimise to our agreed boundaries of control with incredible success. Risk within our boundary (sphere of direct control) is calculated, and it becomes a quantified measure, enabling incentives to be created that provide a mechanism for management control. Risk outside our boundary (indirect control on a longer supply or value chain), is considered as someone else's risk and we are dependent on them to manage it. Such dependencies are vital in modern global businesses. To work with them, we have developed methodology (contracts) and processes (audit) to ensure that we are confident that any risk to us, inside or outside of our direct control, is identified and managed.

However, as leaders, we face three fundamental issues as we move to an economy that serves broader ecosystems, as the boundaries that we are dependent on have become less clear.

1. The quality of the data and implied knowledge we receive from **our direct and dependent* ecosystem,** even if based on audit for financial and non-financial data, is unreliable and increasingly complicated due to different data purposes and ontologies.

2. The quality of the knowledge we receive from **our indirect and interdependent** ecosystem,** even if based on audit for financial and non-financial data, is unreliable and increasingly complicated due to different data purposes and ontologies.

3. Who is responsible and accountable at second and third-order data boundaries? (assuming the first boundary is direct and already in control in our risk model).

* Dependent: balancing being able to achieve by my own effort, with being contingent on or determined by the actions of someone else to make it work.

** Interdependent: combine my efforts with the efforts of others to achieve successful outcomes together, but this does not have to be mutual or controlled.

Risk as a shared belief has wider dependencies

Point 3 above, understanding who is responsible and accountable at second and third-order data boundaries, introduces the concept of these boundaries for broader (inter)dependent ecosystems. This next short section explains where those boundaries are and why they matter in the context of a business's purpose of moving toward a sustainable ecosystem (ESG).

The figure below expands the dependency thinking into a visual representation. The three axes are **values/ principles** as a focus (self, society, planet earth); who has **accountability/ obligations** (no one, an elected authority such as a director, society, or all of humanity); and **the health of our ecosystems** (prime, secondary, tertiary, and all).

The small blue area shows the limitations of our current shareholder primacy remit, where directors have a fiduciary duty to ensure that their prime business thrives and that value is created for shareholders (stakeholders) at the expense of others. Having a healthy business ecosystem helps with this (competition, choice, diverse risk, margins.) As envisaged by the Business Roundtable, a sustainable ecosystem is represented by the orange area, expanding the directors' remit to more ecosystems and embracing more of a "good for society" set of values, but does not increase director accountability. ESG v1.0 widens the remit to the green area; this step-change expands all current thinking and dependencies of any one player on others on a broader ecosystem. We become sustainable, together.

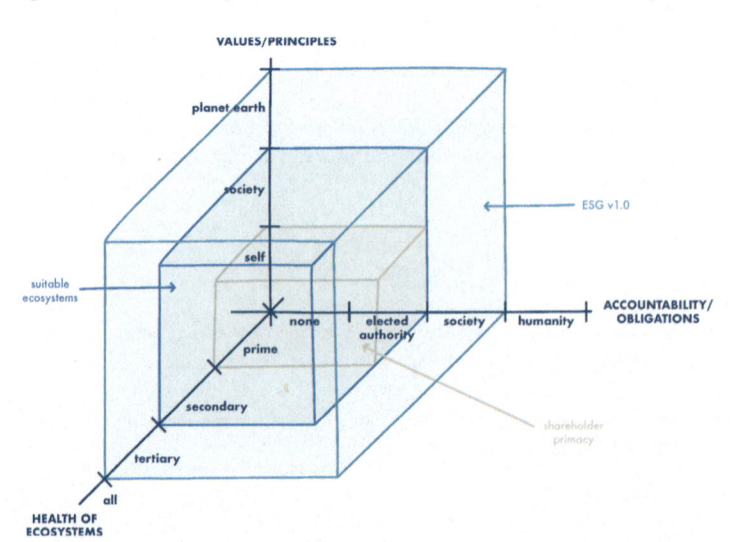

Figure 4: How the impact and likelihood of risk affects management

How is it possible for unidentified risks to exist?

In simple terms, there is no new and unknown risk; however, what is known by one person may not be known by everyone. Risk is hiding in plain sight. As discussed in the previous section, we are expanding our business remits, and as such, are increasingly dependent on others managing their risk to the same level that we manage risk, and sharing data across the ecosystem. This is where **Quantum Risk** arises - at the boundaries, in the long tail of the universe of risk.

The figure below, *The Growing Universe of Risk*, highlights that we are very good at the management of insurable, measurable known: known (identified and shared) risk. We are also very good at un-insurable, measurable (impact, likelihood, knowledge) and known: unknown risk, mainly because the determined likelihood of occurrence and impact is moderate. Indeed, we have created excellent tools to help mitigate and accept uninsurable, un-measurable unknown: unknown risk. Through mitigation, we accept that the data quality (knowledge) is poor, but the impact of risk is low, as is the likelihood.

Quantum risk is the next step out; it emerges at the boundaries of (inter) dependencies that are created as we create sustainable ecosystems to enable shared data. We are increasingly reliant on data from indirectly related players within our ecosystem, data over which we have no power or control. We have no rights to data and no clue as to its attestation. As it stands, quantum risk does not feature in our current risk models or frameworks and is unimagined to us.

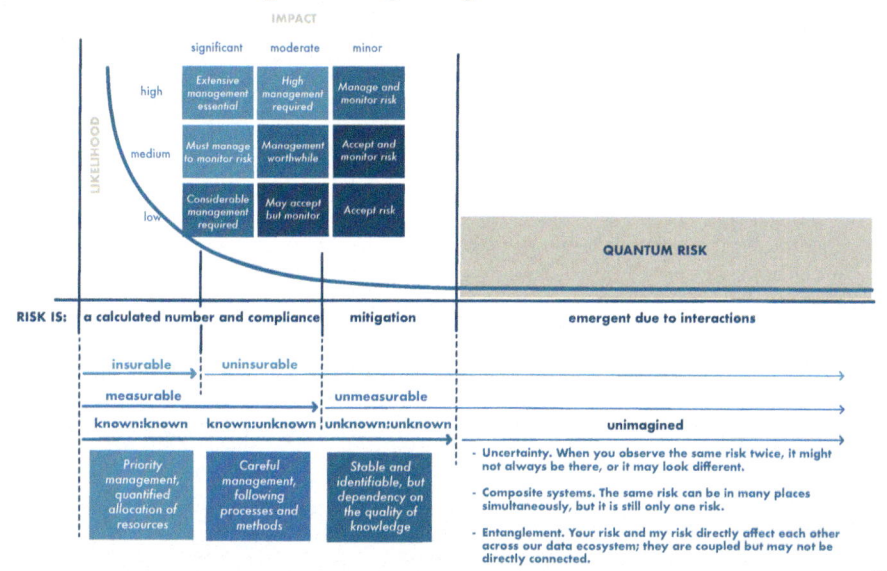

Figure 5: The growing universe of risk

	significant	moderate	minor
high	Extensive management essential	High management required	Manage and monitor risk
medium	Must manage to monitor risk	Management worthwhile	Accept and monitor risk
low	Considerable management required	May accept but monitor	Accept risk

IMPACT / LIKELIHOOD

QUANTUM RISK

RISK IS:	a calculated number and compliance	mitigation	emergent due to interactions
	insurable	uninsurable	
	measurable	unmeasurable	
	known:known	known:unknown	unknown:unknown	unimagined
	Priority management, quantified allocation of resources	Careful management, following processes and methods	Stable and identifiable, but dependency on the quality of knowledge	

- Uncertainty. When you observe the same risk twice, it might not always be there, or it may look different.
- Composite systems. The same risk can be in many places simultaneously, but it is still only one risk.
- Entanglement. Your risk and my risk directly affect each other across our data ecosystem; they are coupled but may not be directly connected.

Business risk vs data risk

Business risk is something that every business has to deal with: Kodak and Nokia maybe not as well as, say, IBM, Barclays or Microsoft. Mobile phone networks should have seen mobile data services coming, and the resulting advent of international voice and video apps that caused the natural decline in SMS, local and international mobile revenue. Most rejected this business risk in 2005, focusing instead on growth in core areas. Ignoring other theories suggested with hindsight, apps such as Signal, WhatsApp and Telegram came about due to the timing of three interrelated advances, which created business risk. These were: device capability, network capability and pricing. Device designers and manufacturers have to keep pushing technology to sell more devices; therefore, device technology will always advance.

Network capacity was always going to increase, and packet-switched capability has massive economies of scale over voice circuits. Large and fast packet circuits were always going to win. Pricing by usage prevents increased usage; on the other hand, bundles work for increasing capacity. For a mobile operator, the objective is to fill the network capacity that is built to maximise ROI – bundles enable this, as do apps that move revenue from one product to the next. This is business risk created by change and dependencies on others in your ecosystem. Quantum risks are a business risk, but they hide in data.

Data risk falls into three buckets:

1. *Data that you collect directly as part of the process of doing business. Critically, you can determine the attestation (provenance and lineage) of the data, and it comes from your own devices, sensors and systems. There is a risk that you don't collect, store, protect, analyse the data, or know if it is true. In truth, this is the front end of the long tail in the universe of risk, and it is precisely what we prioritise. Nothing new here.*

2. Data you collect from third parties that you have a relationship with. Suppliers, partners, collaborators, associates, or public data. Whilst you are likely to have the "rights to use data" (contract), you are unlikely to have "attestation" (provenance and lineage) of the shared data, back to its origin. You will have access to summary or management levels (knowledge and insights), and you should have audit and other contractual agreements to check. There is often an established mutual relationship in which you both share data, and are both dependent on the data quality. The risk is that you don't qualify, check, question or analyse this third party data. In truth, this is another head-end risk of the long tail in the universe of risk, and it is precisely where we invest significant resources. **The exception here is public data, as there is no route to understanding its bias, ontology or purpose. However, public data is not usually used exclusively for decision making, with one exception right now - ESG - which worries me.**

3. Quantum Risk is a data risk in which you have neither control of, or access to, data. Still, this dataset has become critical to decision making as we move towards sustainable business ecosystems, stewardship codes and ESG. However, it requires us to dig into the dark and mysterious world of data ontologies, which we must now quickly unpack.

Ontologies

To explain your reasoning, rationale or position, you need to define how entities are grouped into basic categories that structure your worldview and perspective. If you have a different perspective, you will behave and act differently. Such a structure is called ontology[148] (how we view the world) and is related to epistemology[149] (knowing what is true, and how we have investigated or proved it).

Ontology is a branch of philosophy but is critical in understanding data and information science[150]. It encompasses a representation, formal naming and definition of the categories, properties and relations between the concepts, data and entities that substantiate one, many, or all domains of discourse. Think of data ontology as a way of showing the properties of a subject area and how they are related, by defining a set of concepts and categories that represent the subject.

You would think that with 5,000 years of thinking about this topic we would have one top-level ontology, from which everything would flow. Alas, we don't have one for anything. There is no black-and-white agreed way to look at anything in philosophy, physics, biology, humanities, data, language, sound, knowledge, computers, the climate, behaviour, or any other topic. Therefore, it is safe to assume that your way of describing the world, in your organisation, through data, is different from everyone else in your ecosystem. Those same data points represented in ones and zeros mean completely different things when framed by other ontologies. The worst scenario in a business is different ontologies held within silos, resulting in different world views which may not be common knowledge across the business. Ontologies should be of the focuses of a CDO, which is further explored here[151].

Now to epistemology, which is concerned with the creation of knowledge; focusing on how knowledge is obtained and investigating the most valid ways to reach the "truth". Epistemology essentially determines the relationship between the data, the analyst, and reality, and is rooted in your ontological framework. Different data science teams can have the same dataset and very different views, and to increase complexity, we also have the statistics team. When do you want to hear the truth or lies? This matters when data is shared beyond your company - how do you know what your partners in the business ecosystem think is truthful in their data?

The more we unpack this, the more complicated it gets. As shown in the figure, knowing how you view the world in data does not guarantee that everyone else in your ecosystem has the same view. I have seen very few contracts for data sharing at business data levels in which ontology and mapping schedules are shared. Yes we often share the naming/ data dictionary level, but that is not ontology. **Assuming that shared data has the same purpose for each partner is also quantum risk.** This risk exists at the boundaries, and it only appears when you look closely enough. Imagine you are sharing data[152] on critical systems within your ecosystem, and as you read this, you realise you have not questioned the different worldviews you and your partners have towards collecting, analysing, and reporting data. The event is not the same thing. Remember, at the start, I outlined that we think we know everything about risk. I am in the same starting position. The idea of quantum risk is all new.

Figure 6: Complex Event Processing (CEP) Upper-Level Ontology Modules

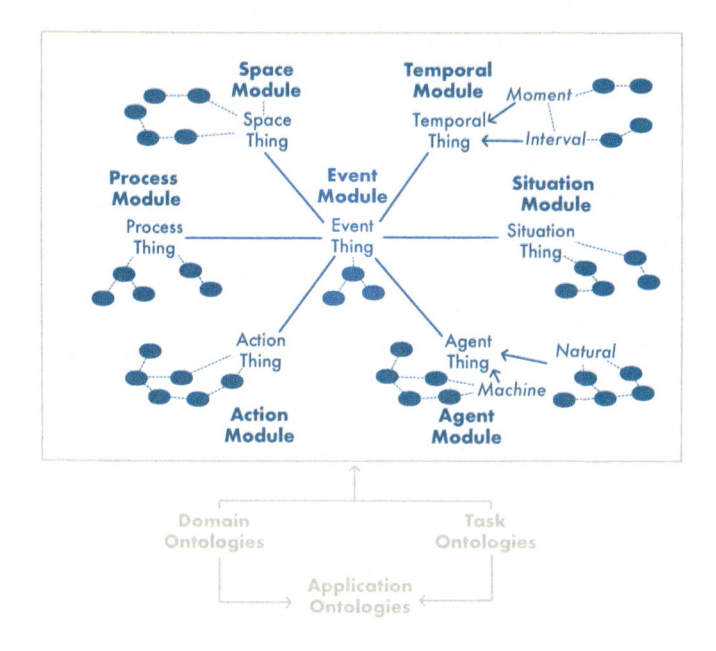

Responses to Quantum Risk

I made two bold claims at the beginning. "The problem we all have with risk is that we think we know it all," and "a bold statement, but quantum risk is new, big, ugly and is already here - it's just that we are willingly blind to it." I wish it were easy, but in fact quantum risk emerges at our digital business boundaries where we share data, and the further from the centre we travel the less attestation and rights we have.

> **The complexity of Quantum Risk creates havoc with our existing frameworks and models as:**
>
> 1. **Uncertainty.** *When you observe the same risk twice, it might not always be there, or it may look different.*
>
> 2. **Composite systems.** *The same risk can be in many places simultaneously, but it is still only one risk.*
>
> 3. **Entanglement.** *Your risk and my risk directly affect each other across our data ecosystem; they are coupled but may not be directly connected.*

Given this, how do we respond? We need to get better at understanding the [purpose of our data](#)[153]; we need to find CDO expertise to help us unpack our data ontologies and rethink what we consider to be our boundaries for commercial purposes, which means revisiting our contracts and terms. One question for those who get this far, is: have you tested how your users understand your Terms and Conditions on data use and privacy? I have never seen it in a test schedule, as it is a barrier and not a value proposition. We tell users to "Click here" fast, and to trust us. This is an obvious gap to investigate as a partner receiving shared data, as you depend on that data, as does your advertising model.

Any good economist or strategist will immediately recognise the opportunity to game data at the boundary. How to create an advantage, and the implications of it, is a whole other topic to unpack.

Figure 7: The response to risk

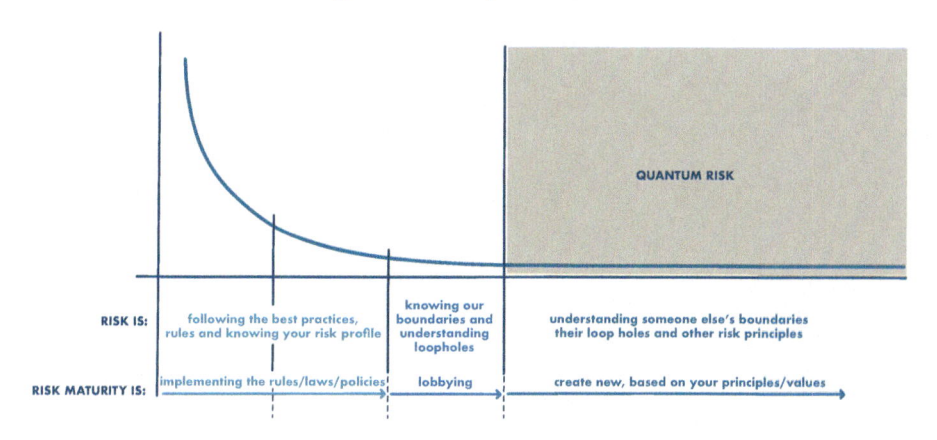

RISK IS:	following the best practices, rules and knowing your risk profile	knowing our boundaries and understanding loopholes	understanding someone else's boundaries their loop holes and other risk principles
RISK MATURITY IS:	implementing the rules/laws/policies	lobbying	create new, based on your principles/values

(QUANTUM RISK)

As a final thought, will your corporation consider Quantum Risk?

If your fellow senior leadership team is focused on the head end of the long tail, you will see a focus on implementing processes that align to regulation, rules, law and policies. You are likely to manage conventional risk very well and be rewarded for doing so, via cascading KPIs. Quantum risk will only be thought about when there are clear best practice examples on display, or there is a visible loss of competitive position.

Corporates with a more mature risk profile know that there are loopholes in risk management, and whilst they have a focus on compliance, they also have a hand in the lobby forums. This is so they can benefit by putting risk onto others and gain an advantage from being the owner of IP when the lobbying is realised as policy. Quantum risk thinking will emerge when there is a clear identification of competitive advantage. The most mature risk leadership teams are creating new thinking to ensure that they are sustainable and are not forced to make retrospective changes (as they would be if they focussed on compliance and had delivery-based KPI-linked bonuses). These are the pioneers in digital and will understand and work with quantum risk first.

Chapter 10

Peak Paradox

Throughout this book, I have asked "how can we make better decisions with data?". Through this journey, we have explored and found that it is not as easy as we imagine and that we always need each other; with each of our differing perspectives, experiences and concepts. With this we are able to expose the available choices, make better decisions, and improve our ability to make judgements.

This final chapter introduces a framework for understanding our personal perspectives that usually create conflict in choice selection and decision making. This framework, Peak Paradox, allows us to explore those perspectives without hostility and conflict.

Why do we need to discover the paradox?

So far in this book, we have unpacked the dependent, independent and interdependent layers that we, as leaders and potential leaders, need to wrestle with if we are to use data to make better decisions. It has already been explained that historical decisions result in existing "shadows, ghosts and incentives" that influence our current ability to make new choices, decisions and judgements. This Chapter presents "Peak Paradox" - a framework to assist in the identification of bias, which stems from experience (the consequences of past decisions) and influences our methods of making decisions.

When in front of a board I ask questions. One of my favourite questions to ask is **"what are you optimising for?"**. And, a bit like asking the "why" question 5 times[154], I continue to interrogate "what we are optimising for" until it exposes the differences in what each individual is personally optimising for, and their understanding of what the company, business, organisation, or institution is optimising for. This process can quickly become hostile, so the purpose of Peak Paradox is to help us determine what we are optimising for, and then identify barriers and remove the hurdles in reaching a Northstar - without the conflict. If we cannot see or find the "paradoxes" created by individual opinion, it highlights that there is a gap in our understanding, or that our bias is so extreme that we only believe in the specific model that frames our thinking.

A paradox is...

A paradox emerges when a seemingly absurd or contradictory statement or proposition, when investigated, may prove to be well-founded or true. A paradox is created when the same evidence/ data/ facts, when viewed from different perspectives, give contradictory conclusions.

Whereas, a dilemma is about competing choices, where you must weigh up a range of advantages and disadvantages, forcing an either/ or situation. As executives and leaders, we should remain curious and expose both the paradoxes and dilemmas... and more.

A Paradox also occurs when a person or thing combines contradictory features or qualities. A Paradox is a statement or proposition which, despite sound (or apparently sound) reasoning from acceptable premises, leads to a conclusion that seems logically unacceptable or self-contradictory.

In this context, when data or information is presented, it is often based on a set of assumptions that are generic, and never read or challenged. The Peak Paradox framework enables executive management and leadership teams to take back ownership of risk and assumptions so that they can together explore and find the paradox about the decision they are being asked to make, which leads to better outcomes.

The BEIGE button is true

The BLUE button is false

Figure 1: What is a paradox?

"Purpose" must have a Northstar if it is to be realised

Whilst for an individual, purpose makes sense, purpose as a "reason or rationale" is full of paradoxes when applied at scale. Humanity cannot agree on a unified "Human Purpose," and there are not sufficient resources nor the time available to enable us to optimise for every individual's perspective. This creates a need for choices and decisions around allocation and priority, and such limits and boundaries create paradoxes and dilemmas.

As humanity, we realise there are many "purposes", as every one of us uses our resources (time, and money - both made up human constructs) to realise what we think or believe is important. Therefore, we have to find a way to compromise and be able to allocate limited resources. In business, a Northstar allows us to optimise in, seemingly, the same direction and go on the same journey together, papering over subtle differences, and enabling tensions to be lived with. All we have actually achieved by doing this is an alignment towards a single optimised ideal at the expense of "others", and found the team who also agree on these compromises. For some reason, we find some compromises easier than others, which means we tend to follow a defined path and align with others who also cannot compromise on the same issues.

"Smart leaders" apparently make yearly resolutions and set quarterly milestones, charting progress against ambitious plans and goals. Whereas, "wise leaders" build from a foundational purpose that creates a compelling vision, driving action — not just for that year, but for the rest of their lives. That purpose helps find and lock onto a Northstar, which provides direction when the path ahead is hazy; humility when arrogance announces false victory; and inspiration when the outlook seems bleak.

That feeling of certainty does not go away as the data (or something that you instinctively know) is telling you that you have compromised on the "better" outcome ("best" does not exist). Whilst we cannot touch, see or feel what it is that frustrates us and holds us back, we know we would like something that helps us gain clarity and understanding. As a leader, you must look for the small signals in paradoxes or you will remain in your existing mental framing or model, not realising that you are optimising for something that may in fact be the wrong thing. This is why the Peak Paradox framework is useful. Without it, dilemmas, because of human nature, provide easy distractions.

"My intentions are good, so please don't let me be misunderstood" are lyrics written by Bennie Benjamin, Horace Ott and Sol Marcus for Nina Simone, who recorded the first version of the song *Don't let me be misunderstood* in 1964. It is an ideal reminder that opinions can easily be translated by others, even with the best of intentions, creating dilemmas and paradoxes.

Irrespective of how much data analysis, information and insight is available, there is always more than one possible outcome, consequence, or conclusion. Peak Paradox frames and identifies systems and processes, and how they can work to undermine the good decisions and judgements that management and leadership teams make. The Peak Paradox framework is designed to help us understand why some decisions taken do not create the best outcome (optimised for the resources available), by providing clarity on the compromises each of us brings to a team decision. What is truly unique is that Peak Paradox helps unpack "why" – without creating tension or conflict.

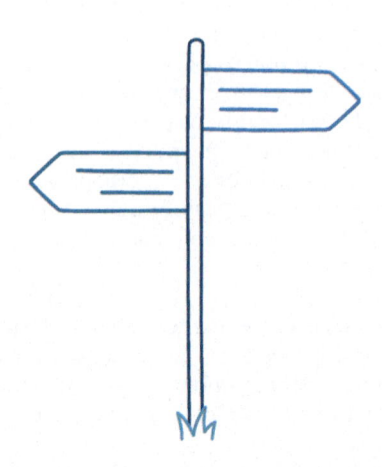

Perception is a strange thing

I can view the situation from your shoes or mine; we see the same liquid in a glass quite uniquely, one-half full and the other half empty. Our imaginations will fill in the missing details very differently. When light creates a shadow in two dimensions of a three-dimensional object, we lose detail and add our own interruption.
Perspective matters.

If we can shift ourselves to understand something from a different perspective, I believe we can move from believing in the "right" or "wrong" of an opinion to being able to think and act differently. This allows us to seek out and find paradoxes, live with them, and lead teams in times of uncertainty and complexity.

Peak Paradox is a framework designed to embrace many perspectives and will expose the differences in our biases, opinions and values. Tension is always present, as we all have unique perspectives – but this framework is non-confrontational and avoids defensive reactions, such as blame, conflict and righteousness.

Figure 2: The Peak Paradox framework

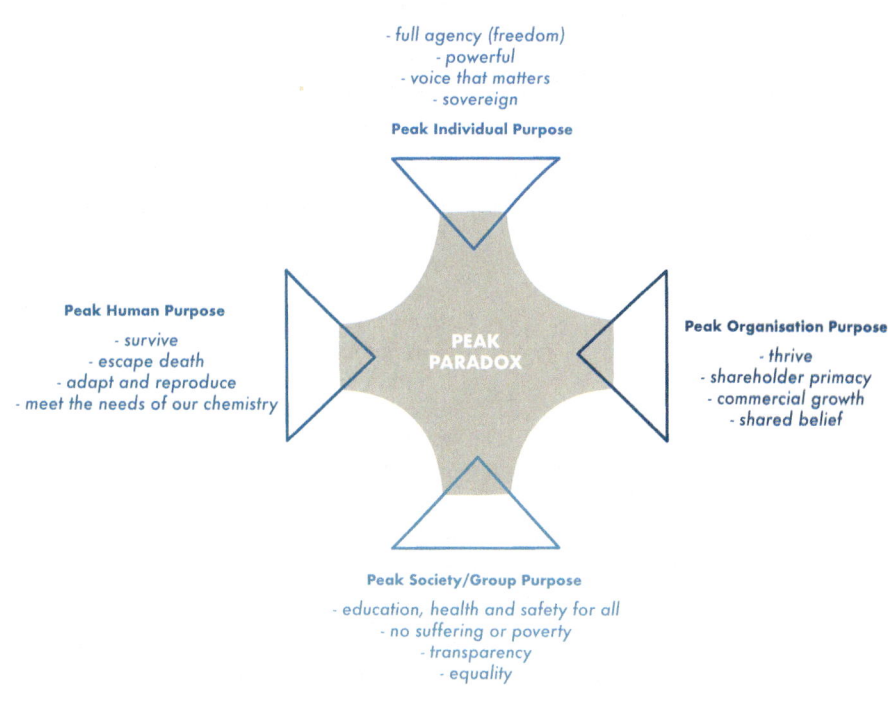

Peak Individual Purpose
- full agency (freedom)
- powerful
- voice that matters
- sovereign

Peak Human Purpose
- survive
- escape death
- adapt and reproduce
- meet the needs of our chemistry

PEAK PARADOX

Peak Organisation Purpose
- thrive
- shareholder primacy
- commercial growth
- shared belief

Peak Society/Group Purpose
- education, health and safety for all
- no suffering or poverty
- transparency
- equality

Explaining the peaks that form purpose on the Peak Paradox framework

The four outer extremes in the diagram are peaks in their own right. To comprehend the peaks, imagine only holding one narrow view of the purpose at each peak, at the expense of all others. With this focus, there is no conflict or compromise at each peak, as this is the only view that can be held (impossible in reality, but this is just a framework). None can truly exist on their own, as each one would lead to a breakdown of society.

As with the ebb and flow in a predator-prey model[155], when something dominates, something else fades, which itself creates a correction.

The axes are set up so that on the X-axis (horizontal) is the conflict between our human purpose (survive) vs an organisation's (thrive). On the Y-axis (vertical), it is the conflict of an individual (I) vs everyone (us).

1 - Peak individual purpose

Peak individual purpose. At the exclusion of anything else, you are only interested in yourself. Selflessness and narcissism at the extreme. You believe that you are sovereign (not having to ask anyone for permission or forgiveness). Your voice, and everything you say, matters and everyone should agree (dictator). You are all-powerful and can do whatever you want - and you have the freedom and agency to do it.

2 - Peak organisation purpose

Peak organisation purpose. At the exclusion of anything else, the only reason an entity exists is to deliver as much possible "value" to those that matter. In the case of shareholder primacy, employees, customers, and the environment can be exploited. If the organisational purpose is to be the biggest and most efficient beast on the planet, able to deliver enormous returns or results, then it should deliver that at all costs. Simple, clear, without conflict or compromise. It does not matter if the organisation is governmental, charitable or commercial. For a charity or government, the peak will be the purity of its own purpose, where those who vote to support leadership in office set the agenda. It is worth noting that, commercially, the purity of this thinking will extend to the point that rewarding the staff beyond minimum wage would become a compromise. Compliance is met with a minimal standard, ensuring that nothing is wasted.

3 - Peak society/Group purpose

Peak society/ group purpose. At the exclusion of anything else, we must ensure that there is no suffering and poverty for any living thing. Humans must have equal access to education, health and safety. There must be total transparency and equality. Everything is equally shared, and no one has any more power, agency or influence than anyone else.

4 - Peak human purpose

Peak human purpose. At the exclusion of anything else, we are here to escape death - which we do by reproducing as much as we can, with the broadest community we can. We must also adapt as fast as possible. We have to meet our bodies' chemistry requirements to stay alive for as long as possible, to adopt or reproduce at the expense of everything else. Whilst all the peak purposes might be controversial (even to myself), stating that purity of human purpose is rooted in chemistry/biology might not go down very well with many. However, this is a model for framing thinking, so needs to be as pure as possible - please go with it for now.

> **The reason for depicting these extremes as peaks is to articulate that when at the extremes, there is no conflict, no compromise, and no tension.**

Looking at these extremes, it is not that we have to agree with them but to recognise that they can exist. My gut says right-wing politics (given the interpretation of capitalism today, not its original meaning) follows the top edge between Peak Organisation Purpose and Peak Individual Purpose. Depending on the specific view, individuals can identify somewhere along the line, whereas political parties are more complex in their overall position. Left-wing political views (today's interruption, more socialist) follow the bottom right edge between Peak Organisation and Peak Society Purpose.

Again, individual views may hold the line, but political parties are trying to find the right balance of majority votes, commercial activity, tax, redistribution and a fairer society. Applying the same thinking, cults are likely to be positioned along the top-left boundary between Peak Human Purpose and Peak Individual Purpose. In contrast, more fervent religious movements will tend towards the lower-left boundary between Peak Human and Peak Society Purpose. World religions, like political parties, seek a mass following and therefore are positioned with more paradoxes.

At Peak Paradox; the most central position

Peak Paradox is the melting pot that is the middle of all of the peaks, the place where you are trying to rationalise all the extreme purposes into one acceptable position for everyone. Ultimately, there is no resolution without reaching compromises that will not suit anyone. Peak Paradox is likely to be unsustainable due to the conflicts and compromises required - or may itself be a paradox insomuch as it feels like nothing is there, like the eye of the storm when there is complete calm.

It seems that many great thinkers and philosophers may try to find rest or stillness in this calm at Peak Paradox. There is a battle to reach the place of calm, fighting the storms of opinions, and if you lose that moment of mindfulness, it is straight back into the storm.

> **The unstable nature of standing on the point of a needle. This said:**

- Just because we may agree on the same peak purpose, does not mean we can also agree on how to go about achieving or maintaining it.

- Different peak purposes can have the same principles and values. You start from different peaks and move towards a livable compromise; however, as individuals, you may have the same principles and values, which makes the acceptance of differences more tolerable.

- If there is no paradox or you cannot find one, you are at a boundary edge (where there is the greatest order), or at an extreme peak view.

- At peak paradox, there is the highest disorder in terms of the variety of views.

- It is evident that our society's long list of personality tests seek to identify where you naturally sit right now. You will change and adapt, but there is likely to be a natural affinity that tends towards one or more of the peaks.

- There are over 180 cognitive biases[156] recognised. From this peak paradox diagram, we can unpack that you are unlikely to have them all at the same time, but a subset of them, depending on where you locate yourself.

The reason we are here: how to make better decisions

Stress and tension are created through the cumulative decisions I make in which I compromise from my natural state. This process is part and parcel of being in a society with established norms and values, composed of individuals with freedom and agency. I started analysing this process by writing down many decisions that I have made, and how they map and orientate with the four peak purposes. My examples quickly became very long, complicated and messy, but I identified some trends. I ended up drawing circles to represent different zones.

Figure 3: Peak Paradox and decision making

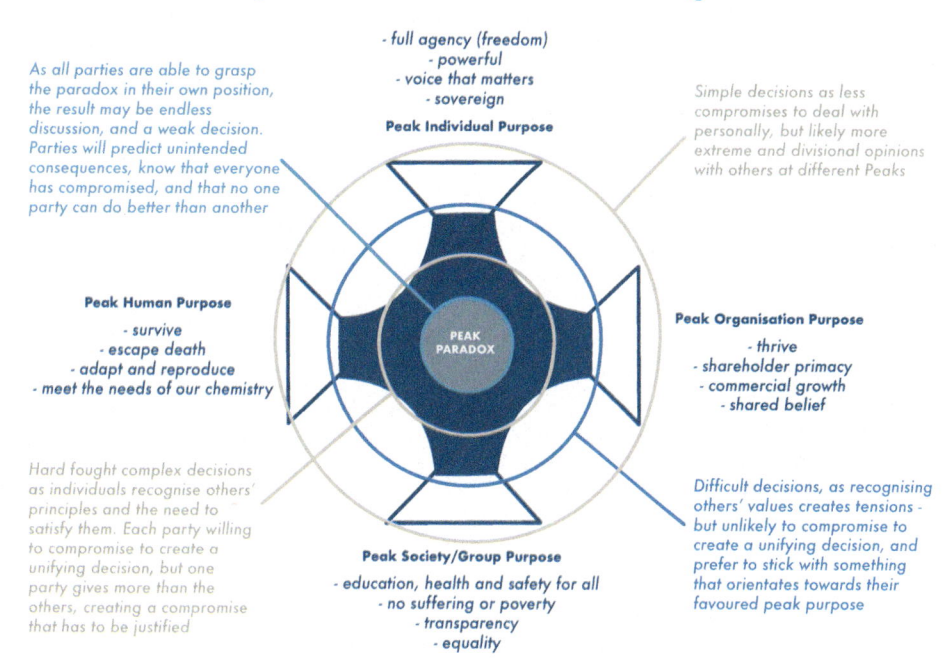

As all parties are able to grasp the paradox in their own position, the result may be endless discussion, and a weak decision. Parties will predict unintended consequences, know that everyone has compromised, and that no one party can do better than another

Peak Individual Purpose
- full agency (freedom)
- powerful
- voice that matters
- sovereign

Simple decisions as less compromises to deal with personally, but likely more extreme and divisional opinions with others at different Peaks

Peak Human Purpose
- survive
- escape death
- adapt and reproduce
- meet the needs of our chemistry

PEAK PARADOX

Peak Organisation Purpose
- thrive
- shareholder primacy
- commercial growth
- shared belief

Hard fought complex decisions as individuals recognise others' principles and the need to satisfy them. Each party willing to compromise to create a unifying decision, but one party gives more than the others, creating a compromise that has to be justified

Peak Society/Group Purpose
- education, health and safety for all
- no suffering or poverty
- transparency
- equality

Difficult decisions, as recognising others' values creates tensions - but unlikely to compromise to create a unifying decision, and prefer to stick with something that orientates towards their favoured peak purpose

The outer beige circle: this represents simple decisions, for which you do not need to compromise. If you need food and water, the whole species' survival is not on top of your plan. Because you are at a peak, there is no consideration of others at different peaks, and affinity is found with the like-minded. Decisions are more extreme and divisional, especially when your opinions are aired beside others at different peaks. Does this sound familiar, like a voyeuristic TV entertainment series or a tabloid media headline?

201

The *inner blue* circle: this starts to include more nuanced decisions, as there is a need to recognise others' values, which creates tensions for everyone - but there is no need to compromise to create a unifying decision. Whilst aware of the conflict, individuals or groups prefer to stick with something that orientates towards their favoured peak purpose.

The *inner beige* circle: getting to the sharp end, these are hard fought for complex decisions where individuals recognise other principles and the need to satisfy more than just themselves to create a better outcome (better decision?). Each party is willing to compromise to create a unifying decision, but one party may have to give up more than the others, which creates a compromise that needs to be justified. Often, if too much is given up, it will not work out - as the justification is lame, and there is a lack of motivation to make it happen. Also, there is more stress and tension for the main compromising party, which can result in them questioning the original decision. It is not a wrong decision; it is just that the compromises move people too far from a natural state. This is the missing third axis in a bilateral negotiation zone, and why the idea of win-win does not play out in reality.

The *smallest blue* circle: all parties can fully grasp the paradox in their own position, and the result may be a weak decision because there are too many super clever people with strong well-reasoned opinions, mixed with too much data. This results in endless discussion, and some people trying to be the brightest in the room. We try to understand everyone too much, but everyone is playing the game. Groups will predict unintended consequences, knowing that everyone is compromised and that no one party can do better than another to create the fairest outcome. Probably the worst decision, and in the long run, it will not create better outcomes - but everyone can live with it for now.

Why purpose is important

I do not doubt that in 7.5 billion years, the earth will be absorbed into the sun en route to becoming a red giant. The earth as a planet will survive to that point, irrespective of what we do and the fate of our species.

Our question is, **"Can we create a good quality of life during that time, given the limitations of the biology we have?"** This is a challenging and complex question, and therefore, we need to think about how we make better decisions using data, in the context of becoming better ancestors. In the context of the problems highlighted above, as at Peak Paradox, we get the most compromise from each party, but the worst decision making and outcomes. And in creating a good quality of life, we need economic activity to enable everyone to have food, water, warmth and downtime.

Suppose we want to provide a good quality of life for generations to come. In that case, we need to focus on decisions made in the outer beige circle, between Peak Human Purpose and Peak Society. There will be many who will not like those decisions - how do we make that work?

Suppose we focus on providing a quality of life for one generation of the powerful few. In that case, we will see decisions focussed in the **inner blue** circle, which will be orientated towards Peak Individual Purpose and Peak Organisation Purpose. How can we make that work?

If we want to provide a good quality of life for everyone alive today, we must realise that we cannot afford to compromise and reach the middle of the Peak Paradox. We have some very tough choices and decisions ahead, and we don't appear to have the forum to have these discussions in the open - probably because we will not like the outcomes. However, if we don't have these discussions, the quality of all of our lives, especially that of future generations, will suffer from our inability to make better decisions. It is why we should use frameworks, like Peak Paradox, to help us make better decisions.

At PeakParadox.com[157] I have begun to unpack how we should look at identity, privacy, teams, incentives, optimising, democracy, ROI, values, regulations, free speech and much more within the framework. I am seeking to provide concrete examples that help us think through these discussions, and create fire.

The opening of this book was called Making Fire, and I wrote: *"In presenting these ten concepts about decision making in uncertain times, the intention is not that I want you to think like me, or that by reading this work you will have the solution to decision making in uncertain times. I want you always to think like you do but have reflected, learnt or honed something about your own framing. This will happen as the book creates sparks, but not agreement. Alignment feels good but leads to group thinking, so I desire that we co-create fire. Like two flints hitting each other to make a spark, your experience and my flow should collide. I will achieve my objective, and value will be created as you realise that you are the fuel. My ask is that when those sparks create goosebumps, you share them with others so that we can all learn from your insights, as this is the oxygen. Together, we will have created a trinity of purifying fire to improve decision making in uncertain times. Ignition, fuel and oxygen."*

I hope the book has created a spark to ignite a new fire, so that I can also continue to learn how to make the right choices, support better decisions and improve my judgements.

References

Chapter 1

Page 26

1	https://towardsdatascience.com/statistics-are-you-bayesian-or-frequentist-4943f953f21b
2	https://en.wikipedia.org/wiki/Cassie_Kozyrkov
3	https://lisafeldmanbarrett.com/
4	https://lisafeldmanbarrett.com/books/seven-and-a-half-lessons-about-the-brain/
5	https://opengovernance.net/quantum-risk-a-wicked-problem-that-emerges-at-the-boundaries-of-our-data-dependency-2dc36dfb21fb
6	https://opengovernance.net/what-occurs-when-physical-beings-transition-to-information-beings-146ea9dcbca3
7	https://opengovernance.net/the-shadowy-hierarch-5780154de92
8	https://opengovernance.net/power-agency-and-influence-a-new-framework-about-complex-relationships-73f5e97295ef

Page 27

9	https://www.decisionprofessionals.com/
10	http://www.sjdm.org/

Page 28

11	https://www.collinsdictionary.com/dictionary/english/choice
12	https://www.oxfordlearnersdictionaries.com/definition/english/choice_1?q=choice
13	https://www.collinsdictionary.com/dictionary/english/decision
14	https://www.oxfordlearnersdictionaries.com/definition/english/decision?q=decision
15	https://www.collinsdictionary.com/dictionary/english/judgment
16	https://www.oxfordlearnersdictionaries.com/definition/english/judgement?q=judgment

Page 33

17	https://opengovernance.net/data-for-better-decisions-nature-or-nurture-79e6531dbe3a
18	https://opengovernance.net/power-agency-and-influence-a-new-framework-about-complex-relationships-73f5e97295ef
19	https://medium.com/mydata/data-is-data-e2a877cb206b

Page 35

20	https://medium.com/hello-cdo/the-railroad-of-no-choice-a55420cea06f

Page 36

21   https://opengovernance.net/what-99-of-the-public-and-95-of-venture-and-investment-capital-have-got-wrong-69239b4da4f1

Chapter 2

Page 40

22   https://en.wikipedia.org/wiki/Yes_Minister

Page 41

23   https://www.globe-project.eu/en

Page 43

24   https://theconversation.com/is-humanity-doomed-because-we-cant-plan-for-the-long-term-three-experts-discuss-137943

Page 47

25   https://eand.co/our-societies-are-failing-because-their-economies-are-broken-72bb3d378351
26   https://opengovernance.net/the-laws-of-1-how-far-before-you-reach-a-revolution-49bbace4049b
27   https://en.wikipedia.org/wiki/Coconut_shy

Page 48

28   https://en.wikipedia.org/wiki/Volatility,_uncertainty,_complexity_and_ambiguity

Chapter 3

Page 60

29 https://en.wikipedia.org/wiki/Data_lake

Page 63

30 https://www.google.com/search?q=organisational+fit

Page 65

31 https://www.linkedin.com/in/mikesmith9/

Chapter 4

Page 72

32 https://www.regulatoryaffairsawards.org/

Page 74

33 https://en.wikipedia.org/wiki/Rights

Chapter 5

Page 80

34 https://en.wikipedia.org/wiki/Sigmoid_function
35 https://en.wikipedia.org/wiki/Logistic_function
36 https://en.wikipedia.org/wiki/Pierre_Fran%C3%A7ois_Verhulst
37 https://en.wikipedia.org/wiki/Alfred_J._Lotka
38 https://core.ac.uk/download/pdf/7044374.pdf
39 https://en.wikipedia.org/wiki/Technology_adoption_life_cycle

Page 81

40 https://en.wikipedia.org/wiki/Friedman_doctrine

Page 82

41 https://www.hks.harvard.edu/sites/default/files/centers/mrcbg/files/Mayer_2.19.19.transcript.pdf
42 https://www.law.ox.ac.uk/business-law-blog/blog/2020/11/value-creation-and-corporate-governance
43 https://www.businessroundtable.org/business-roundtable-redefines-the-purpose-of-a-corporation-to-promote-an-economy-that-serves-all-americans
44 https://www.frc.org.uk/investors/uk-stewardship-code
45 https://www.legislation.gov.uk/ukpga/2006/46/section/172/2011-04-22
46 https://www.linkedin.com/in/simonwardley/
47 https://medium.com/wardleymaps
48 https://www.youtube.com/watch?v=JMlFv2Sod54
49 https://blog.gardeviance.org/2015/08/on-diffusion-and-evolution.html

Page 83

50 https://en.wikipedia.org/wiki/Ubiquity
51 https://en.wikipedia.org/wiki/Certainty
52 https://www.mydigitalfootprint.com/2020/09/pathways-to-general-ai-unimagined.html

Page 85

53 https://corpgov.law.harvard.edu/2019/08/22/so-long-to-shareholder-primacy/
54 https://www.law.ox.ac.uk/business-law-blog/blog/2020/11/value-creation-and-corporate-governance
55 https://www.mydigitalfootprint.com/2020/07/preparing-directors-for-duties-and.html

Page 87

56 https://en.wikipedia.org/wiki/Corporate_governance
57 https://en.wikipedia.org/wiki/Cadbury_Report
58 https://en.wikipedia.org/wiki/Corporate_governance#Sarbanes%E2%80%93Oxley_Act
59 https://en.wikipedia.org/wiki/Governance,_risk_management,_and_compliance

Page 89

60 https://www.mydigitalfootprint.com/2020/11/the-changing-nature-of-business.html
61 https://www.mydigitalfootprint.com/2020/09/leadership-for-organisational-fitness.html
62 https://www.mydigitalfootprint.com/2020/11/data-portability-mobility-sharing.html

Page 90

63 https://www.mydigitalfootprint.com/2020/07/what-changes-when-you-consider.html
64 https://www.digital20.com/

Chapter 6

Page 95

65 https://www.etymonline.com/word/rule

Page 99

66 https://en.wikipedia.org/wiki/Alexander_Fraser_Tytler,_Lord_Woodhouselee

Page 101

67 https://en.wikipedia.org/wiki/Dignity
68 https://en.wikipedia.org/wiki/Subsidiarity_(European_Union)
69 https://en.wikipedia.org/wiki/Solidarity
70 https://en.wikipedia.org/wiki/Covenant_theology
71 https://en.wikipedia.org/wiki/Sustainability
72 https://en.wikipedia.org/wiki/Common_good
73 https://en.wikipedia.org/wiki/Stewardship
74 https://en.wikipedia.org/wiki/Declaration_of_Principles_on_Equali

Page 104

75 https://www.mydigitalfootprint.com/2019/01/data-is-data-it-is-not-oil-or-gold-or.html
76 https://ico.org.uk/for-organisations/guide-to-data-protection/guide-to-the-general-data-protection-regulation-gdpr/principles/
77 https://gdpr-info.eu/art-5-gdpr/
78 https://medium.com/@tonyfish/power-agency-and-influence-a-new-framework-about-complex-relationships-73f5e97295ef

Page 105

79 https://www.mydigitalfootprint.com/2020/11/data-portability-mobility-sharing.html

Chapter 7 - Part one

Page 110

80 https://en.wikipedia.org/wiki/Being_Digital

Page 111

81 https://en.wikipedia.org/wiki/Identity
82 https://en.wikipedia.org/wiki/Rivalry_(economics)
83 https://en.wikipedia.org/wiki/Excludability

Page 112

84 https://www.penguin.co.uk/books/285465/the-mind-is-flat-by-chater-nick/9780241208779
85 https://doc.searls.com/2020/02/10/commons/

Page 113

86 https://doc.searls.com/
87 https://papers.ssrn.com/sol3/papers.cfm?abstract_id=2916489

Page 114

88 https://phmuseum.com/projects/usus-fructus-abusus
89 https://en.wikipedia.org/wiki/Commons
90 https://en.wikipedia.org/wiki/Right_of_way

Page 115

91 https://en.wikipedia.org/wiki/Physical_health
92 https://en.wikipedia.org/wiki/Social_status
93 https://en.wikipedia.org/wiki/Uncertainty

Chapter 7 - Part two

Page 120

94	Page 106 - Chapter 7 (part one)
95	https://www.linkedin.com/in/theodoralau/
96	https://www.linkedin.com/in/hughmacleod/

Page 121

97	https://www.investopedia.com/terms/f/fiatmoney.asp6

Page 124

98	https://www.linkedin.com/in/scott-david-35a5887/

Chapter 7 - Part three

Page 130

99	https://en.wikipedia.org/wiki/Judgment_of_Solomon
100	https://en.wikipedia.org/wiki/Archetype
101	https://link.springer.com/chapter/10.1007/978-3-319-91743-6_2

Chapter 8 - Part one

Page 140

102 https://www.waterstones.com/book/making-evil/dr-julia-shaw/9781786891327
103 https://www.drjuliashaw.com/

Page 141

104 https://www.legislation.gov.uk/ukpga/2006/46/section/172

Page 142

105 https://www.cdbb.cam.ac.uk/files/a_survey_of_top-level_ontologies_lowres.pdf

Page 143

106 https://medium.com/hello-cdo
107 https://www.mydigitalfootprint.com/2020/11/data-portability-mobility-sharing.html?q=portability
108 https://tonyfish.medium.com/quantum-risk-a-wicked-problem-that-emerges-at-the-boundaries-of-our-data-dependency-2dc36dfb21fb

Page 144

109 https://en.wikipedia.org/wiki/Paradigm_shift

Page 146

110 https://medium.com/dataseries/training-machine-learning-models-to-ask-the-right-questions-b6235dd5872b

Chapter 8 - Part two

Page 150

111 https://www.researchgate.net/figure/The-Data-Frame-Theory-of-Sensemaking-The-Data-Frame-Theory-of-Sensemaking-consists-of_fig2_253238532

Page 153

112 https://opengovernance.net/updating-board-paper-for-a-data-attestation-section-db59d736ccc5
113 Page 116 - Chapter 7
114 Page 134 - chapter 8

Page 154

115 https://imgs.xkcd.com/comics/standards.png
116 https://en.wikipedia.org/wiki/Ontology
117 https://en.wikipedia.org/wiki/Metaphysics
118 https://en.wikipedia.org/wiki/Upper_ontology

Page 156

119 Page 124 - Chapter 7

Page 159

120 https://en.wikipedia.org/wiki/Social_capital

Chapter 8 - Part three

Page 164

121	https://www.youtube.com/watch?v=9ZorLUKe4Jg
122	https://www.bbc.co.uk/programmes/m000b1v2
123	https://en.wikipedia.org/wiki/Human_Compatible
124	http://www.cpt.univ-mrs.fr/~rovelli/
125	https://www.bbc.com/reel/video/p086tg3k/the-physics-that-suggests-we-have-no-free-will

Page 166

| 126 | https://svs.gsfc.nasa.gov/vis/a000000/a003800/a003822/magnetic_field_cover.png |

Page 168

127	https://en.wikipedia.org/wiki/Quark
128	https://en.wikipedia.org/wiki/Gluon
129	https://www.home.cern/science/accelerators/large-hadron-collider
130	https://en.wikipedia.org/wiki/Quantum

Page 169

| 131 | https://en.wikipedia.org/wiki/Uncertainty_principle |

Page 172

132	https://www.statisticshowto.com/probability-and-statistics/hypothesis-testing/
133	https://www.statisticshowto.com/probability-and-statistics/probability-main-index/
134	https://www.statisticshowto.com/probability-and-statistics/statistics-definitions/mean-median-mode/#mean
135	https://www.statisticshowto.com/probability-and-statistics/standard-deviation/
136	https://www.statisticshowto.com/probability-and-statistics/confidence-interval/

Page 173

137 https://www.linkedin.com/in/scott-david-35a5887/

Page 174

138 https://www.mydigitalfootprint.com/2020/09/leadership-for-organisational-fitness.html
139 https://medium.com/@tonyfish/the-accumulation-of-an-executives-successfulness-with-kpi-measures-is-not-an-indicator-of-a-future-a170409a0c8a
140 https://en.wikipedia.org/wiki/John_Maynard_Keynes

Chapter 9

Page 178

141 https://www.linkedin.com/in/peadar-duffy-b47360a/
142 https://www.linkedin.com/feed/update/urn:li:activity:6762051599817875456/

Page 179

143 https://www.businessroundtable.org/business-roundtable-redefines-the-purpose-of-a-corporation-to-promote-an-economy-that-serves-all-americans
144 https://www.blackrock.com/uk/individual/larry-fink-ceo-letter
145 https://assets.publishing.service.gov.uk/government/uploads/system/uploads/attachment_data/file/852960/brydon-review-final-report.pdf

Page 182

146 Page 116 - Chapter 7
147 https://www.mydigitalfootprint.com/2021/02/what-is-purpose-of-data-v2.html

Page 187

148 https://en.wikipedia.org/wiki/Ontology
149 https://en.wikipedia.org/wiki/Epistemology
150 https://en.wikipedia.org/wiki/Ontology_(information_science)

Page 188

151   https://medium.com/hello-cdo
152   https://www.mydigitalfootprint.com/2020/11/data-portability-mobility-sharing.html

Page 190

153   Page 116 - Chapter 7

Chapter 10

Page 194

154   https://en.wikipedia.org/wiki/Five_whys

Page 198

155   https://medium.com/hello-cdo/predator-prey-models-to-model-users-9ed717fa548f

Page 200

156   https://www.peakparadox.com/post/peak-paradox

Page 203

157   https://www.peakparadox.com/blog

The last word

I want to extend my gratitude to the team behind the book Decision Making in Uncertain Times. The publication of this work was only possible with the dedication and expertise of designer [Helen Fairlie](#) and editor [Phoebe Jarvis](#).

To Helen, your creative vision and attention to detail have brought the pages of my book to life. Your design throughout captures the essence of the book's content. Your ability to translate abstract ideas into stunning visuals is remarkable, and I couldn't be happier with the final result. Thank you.

To Phoebe, your meticulous work ensured that the text flowed seamlessly, free from errors, and with a consistent tone and style. Your insightful suggestions and constructive feedback improved the clarity and coherence of the content. Your commitment to enhancing the manuscript has made this book a more polished and reader-friendly product. Thank you.

The final word

Thank you to my wife, Nicky, who keeps me grounded in the times I am found drifting with the stars. To my daughter Ellie and husband, Freddie, thank you for giving me wisdom and insight as to how the next generation thinks, sees and understands a sustainable world. To my daughter Emilia and partner, Alex, thank you for forcing me to think about governance in biological systems and for providing a portal into other expertise, ideas and domains.

Finally, for my dad, MEF, who left me with many questions - but I particularly appreciate these. Questions such as "Who in this meeting is having their thinking supervised?" and "Who is supervising that person's thinking?". Brilliant, curious and inquisitive questions that help me make better decisions in uncertain times.

About the author

Tony Fish is neuro-minority and a leading expert on decisionmaking in uncertain environments, governance and entrepreneurship. C-ENG, FIET, FBCS, FCIM, FRSA.

He thrives in complex, ground-breaking & uncertain environments, bringing proven judgement and decision-making skills with cross-sectorial experience. His 30-year track record of sense-making and foresight means he has been ahead on several technical revolutions. His enthusiasm and drive are contagious & inspiring, especially for wicked problems.

In addition to speaking at events on leadership, future trends, and data, he has written and published five books. Tony remains a visiting Fellow at Henley Business School for Entrepreneurship and Innovation, EIR at Bradford School of Management, teaches at London Business School and the London School of Economics in AI and Ethics and is an EC expert for Big Data.

Having observed that it is easy for Board members to become removed from the reality of life, and to remain grounded, Tony spends eight days a month providing hands-on practical skills (as a handyperson) in his local community through "help the aged", the local hospice, directly with local residents and as a volunteer at the local repair shop.

Printed in Great Britain
by Amazon